BRADFORD
COLLEGE
LIBRARY

Democratisation Processes in Africa:
Problems and Prospects

Democratisation Processes in Africa: Problems and Prospects

**Edited by
Eshetu Chole and Jibrin Ibrahim**

CODESRIA BOOK SERIES

Democratisation Processes in Africa: Problems and Prospects

First published in 1995 by CODESRIA

Copyright © CODESRIA

CODESRIA is the Council for the Development of Social Science Research in Africa, headquartered in Senegal. It is an independent organisation whose principal objectives are facilitating research, promoting research-based publishing and creating multiple fora geared towards the exchange of views and information among African scholars. Its correspondence address is: B.P. 3304, Dakar, Senegal.

ISBN 2-86978-052-4

Cover designed by Ousmane Ndiaye Dago
Typeset by Marie Therese Coron-Diouf, CODESRIA
Distributor: The African Books Collective Ltd.,
The Jam Factory - 27 Park End Street,
Oxford OX1 1HU England

CODESRIA would like to express its gratitude to the Swedish Agency for Research Cooperation (SAREC), the Rockefeller Foundation, the International Development Research Centre (IDRC), the Ford Foundation, the Norwegian Ministry of Foreign Affairs and the Danish Agency for International Development (DANIDA) for support of its research and publication activities

Notes on Contributors

Archie Mafeje was educated at the Universities of Cape Town and Cambridge. He has had a distinguished academic career, including most recently the Chair of Sociology, American University, Cairo. His recent publications include the *Theory and Ethnography of African Social Formations* (1991 CODESRIA).

Eboe Hutchful is visiting Professor at the African Studies Department of Wayne State University, Detroit. He is co-author with G. Smith of *Democratisation and Popular Participation* (North-South Institute 1992).

Eshetu Chole is an Associate Professor in the Department of Economics, Addis Ababa University. He is the co-author of *Profiles of the Ethiopian Economy* (1969) and has edited many publications. He has published numerous articles on various aspects of the Ethiopian economy.

Jibrin Ibrahim is a Senior Lecturer in the Department of Political Science, Ahmadu Bello University (Zaria, Nigeria). He has a doctorate from the University of Bordeaux on Nigerian party politics and has published widely in English and in French on democratisation, pluralism and religious conflict.

Kankwenda Mbaya, formerly a Professor at the Kinshasa Institute of Advanced Communication Techniques (UNIKIN), is now an economist with the UNDP. His recent publications include: *Zaire: What Destiny?* ed. (1993 CODESRIA).

Mahmood Mamdani, Executive Director, Centre for Basic Research, Kampala, Uganda and Associate Professor, Department of Political Science, Makerere University, Kampala. Author of *Imperialism and Fascism in Uganda* 1984); Africa World Press; co-editor of *Academic Freedom in Africa* 1994 (with Mamadou Diouf) Dakar, CODESRIA; and *African Studies in Social Movements in Africa* with Ernest Wamba-dia-Wamba (1995 CODESRIA).

Peter Anyang' Nyong'o has written widely on African politics and processes of development. His recent publications include: *Thirty Years of Independence in Africa: The Lost Decades?* Nairobi, (1992, Academy of Science Publishers).

Thandika Mkandawire is Executive Secretary of the Council for the Development of Social Science Research in Africa (CODESRIA). His research interests are on food and agricultural issues, sub-regional cooperation, social movements in Africa. He is co-editor of *The State and Agriculture in Africa* with Naceur Bourenane (1987 CODESRIA), *Africa's Recovery in the 1990s: From Stagnation and Adjustment to Human Development*, with G. A. Cornia and R. Vander Hoeven (1992 UNICEF).

Contents

1. Introduction 1
   Eshetu Chole

2. Theory of Democracy and the African Discourse:
   Breaking Bread with my Fellow-travellers 5
   Archie Mafeje

3. Discourses on Democracy in Africa 29
   Peter Anyang' Nyong'o

4. Democratic Theory and Democratic Struggles 43
   Mahmood Mamdani

5. The Economic Crisis, Adjustment and Democracy
   in Africa 63
   Kankwenda M'Baya

6. Adjustment, Political Conditionality and
   Democratisation in Africa 81
   Thandika Mkandawire

7. The International Dimensions of the Democratisation
   Process in Africa 100
   Eboe Hutchful

8. Democratic Transition in Africa: The Challenge of a
   New Agenda — Concluding Remarks 120
   Jibrin Ibrahim

1. Introduction

Eshetu Chole

The papers that appear in this volume were selected from more than twenty-five contributions made at the Seventh General Assembly of the Council for the Development of Social Science Research in Africa (CODESRIA), which was held between 10 and 14 February 1992, the theme being 'Democratisation Processes in Africa: Problems and Prospects'.

In making the selections, the editors decided to exclude papers devoted to specific country studies, partly because their inclusion would have made the volume excessively bulky and partly because it was felt that publishing the general papers only would make it possible to focus on issues of continent-wide significance. Of the general papers, those that have been included here are the ones which the editors felt made the most substantive contributions. While the papers selected address some of the most salient problems pertaining to democratisation in contemporary Africa, they by no means do so exhaustively. They do, however, provide plenty of food for thought.

The rationale for devoting the Seventh General Assembly of CODESRIA to issues of democratisation should be self-evident. Developments in the late 1980s and early 1990s in one African country after another brought to the centre of the political stage a wide variety of social forces that seriously challenged the existing order, in some cases rocking it to its very foundations. Regimes once considered well-entrenched were buffeted by forces they could neither comprehend nor control, and some of them were subsequently consigned to the history books.

To be sure, the collapse of erstwhile apparently impregnable regimes and systems was not a uniquely African phenomenon. In fact, the 'wind of change' — which was more of a hurricane this time — wreaked havoc on regime after regime in the former Soviet Union and countries within its orbit. There is thus an obvious link between the global and African phenomena, although one should be wary of hastily seeking to establish direct cause-effect relationships between the two.

Whatever the impact of the international environment may be, it seems that democratisation is firmly on the African political agenda. What the significance of this phenomenon on a historical scale will be, only the future will tell. How, for instance, would its impact compare with that of the process of decolonisation of the early 1960s? Those of us who lived through those heady times will recall what euphoria they generated and what expectations they created. That euphoria and those expectations, as is only too well-known, turned out to be short-lived, and the legacy of a generation of 'flag independence' has been nothing but a 'harvest of sorrow'.

Euphoria has now been rekindled by the contemporary wave of democratisation, which at one time seemed destined to engulf the whole continent. Now, with the collapse of apartheid in South Africa, one might say it has assumed a new dimension. How many of those assembled at the Seventh General Assembly of CODESRIA had realistically expected that apartheid would be shattered in a matter of two years? Indeed, how many who were adults in the 1960s could have predicted the emergence of majority rule during their lifetimes?

Therefore, the euphoria is understandable, even if not fully justifiable. The task of African social scientists goes beyond joining the chorus of jubilation and demands at least an understanding of the nature of the democratisation process, its strengths and limitations, as well as its prospects. For the questions the new phase poses are legion. While not all of them can be effectively addressed, it behoves African intellectuals, working individually and collectively, to seek answers to the most pressing ones, some of which are the following:

Is what is taking place democratisation in content or merely in form, or more exactly, how much substance and how much form does it involve? If there is substance in it, what are the features that lend it this character? If it is more form than content, what justifies the celebrations, which have sometimes been highly vocal? What are the limitations and contradictions of this process? What are the social forces — internal as well as external — behind it? How compatible or otherwise are the interests of these forces? What is the link between economic reform and democratisation? What guarantees, if any, are there against the reversibility of the process?

If African social scientists do not grapple with these and a host of other related questions and merely succumb to the euphoria of the moment, they will have failed in what is probably their most important task of the day.

An obvious starting point for this enterprise is a critical assessment of the first three decades of the post-colonial era. While it brooks no dispute that this period represented generalised failure of gigantic proportions in the political, economic and social spheres, there is little agreement on the underlying causes of the failure. Was the independence project a 'false start' from the beginning, or was it hijacked mid-course? What lessons are to be drawn by taking stock of that period, lessons which could be put to good use in understanding the present?

At least one lesson it suggests would seem to be that uncritical adulation of the current phenomenon of democratisation is unwarranted. That this statement is not gratuitous should be of some of the frequent—and at times hasty—characterisation of some of the new African regimes as democratic. They may well deserve the appellation, but this is something that has to be demonstrated, not taken at face value. Thus, it is not sufficient for a regime to be voted into power by popular elections for it to be dubbed democratic. While such regimes undoubtedly represent an advance over those that had perpetuated themselves in office — with or without the benefit of fake elections, it takes more than free elections to bestow the democratic title on any given regime. After all, the essence of democracy resides in the relationship between the state and the people, especially on how much control the latter have over the former.

Insisting on this point is not tantamount to demanding perfection from the new regimes. That would be both utopian and irresponsible. While every effort should be made to enhance such positive characteristics as these regimes may possess, there is also need for a critical examination of their limitations, a task which should be viewed as part of the social responsibility of the African intellectual. After all, African society will be served not by uncritical acclaim of every departure from the old ways, but by a sustained and critical analysis of the unfolding situation. The point, quite simply, is that there should be no room for uncritical acceptance of whatever appears new.

A corollary of this point is that, at the other extreme, there should be no room either for a summary dismissal of the political changes as merely cosmetic and hence inconsequential. Social struggles are fought—and won — by stages, each stage being richly textured with advances and setbacks. Gains that appear minor when viewed in isolation may cumulatively add up to achievements that cannot be ignored. This is also true of democratisation experiments in Africa. That they are flawed in may respects is obvious. They are partial, because they have yet to make a dent in several countries that have remained unresponsive to them. Even where they appear to have made much progress, their sustainability remains subject to question. But these facts do not justify their disparagement, for disparagement could easily play into the hands of the vested interest of the status quo. The task, once again, is one of critical understanding. And critical understanding requires careful study, not blanket dismissal.

One thing that is certain is that struggles for democracy in Africa, like all such struggles, are not going to be easy or quickly consummated. Circumstances are bound to vary from country to country, and it is the task of analysts to seek what is common to all experiences without being insensitive to specific country situations. It is also imperative for African social scientists to distinguish between the purely ephemeral aspects of the transition to democracy and those of a more enduring nature.

One aspect of the transition that makes it especially difficult to grasp is the peculiar confluence of the political and economic agendas, an issue addressed by a number of papers in this book. Is it accidental that the tasks of democratisation and those of economic reform have been posed at one and the same time? What exactly is the relationship between democratic governance and economic reform? More specifically, is democracy a prerequisite for attaining economic growth? Of course whoever answers this question in the affirmative, one might ask how they would explain this new orthodoxy after having argued for decades that a 'strong state' is absolutely indispensable for engineering growth, i.e., that democratic principles have to be sacrificed at the altar of growth?

For Africa, a continent that has known very little of either, this question is all the more relevant because economic reform is now equated with standard structural adjustment programs, programs which are not only essentially exogenous in conception but have also conspicuously failed to deliver on their promises. What latitudes exist for regimes that have been brought to power by broad social movements but are literally coerced into implementing programs that set them on a collision course with those forces on the backs of which they rode to power? And what substance does the claim of national sovereignty have in such circumstances?

These questions — and experiences to date — suggest that there is much that is fragile in the democratisation project in Africa today. As in the case of all social struggles, its ultimate outcome is difficult to predict in advance. While it opens new vistas, it is also subject to formidable constraints which make its future course highly unpredictable.

This is why it is absolutely essential for African social scientists to study the democratisation process in its complex dynamics. The papers in this collection do make a tentative beginning in this regard. The authors themselves would be the first to admit that their analyses are preliminary and partial, and therefore in need of refinement. But it cannot be denied that there is much in these pages that will stimulate dialogue, by no means an insignificant achievement.

2. Theory of Democracy and the African Discourse: Breaking Bread with my Fellow-travellers

Archie Mafeje

The Grammar of Theory and Politics

At the risk of being accused of pedantry we must insist on the logic of language and its predications in our intellectual discourse, if not for ourselves, then for the sake of future generations. Given our circumstances, this is said with all the gravity it deserves. For instance, it is not unworthy to point out that it is one thing to endow theory with immanent qualities and another to perceive of theory as a tool for making apparent the meaning of its object of analysis, e.g. 'democracy', which is at once a concept and a socio-historical process. Likewise, while discourse might be predicated on a particular object, e.g. 'theory', it is worth noting that by so doing it does not confer upon theory any ontological attributes but at best aims to illuminate its possible connotations under determinate conditions. So will it be with African discourse on theory (used as a collective noun) of democracy.

Since Greek times there has been only one definition of 'democracy', namely, rule by the 'demos', i.e., the people. But throughout history there have been people and 'non-people'. This fact marks the historicity of the concept of 'democracy', which often seems to be lost sight of in current debates in Africa. Plato's distinctions between men of 'gold', 'silver' and 'copper' and Aristotle's between philosophers and the others were not without significance. But Greek and even Roman antiquity need not concern us much here.

For modern definitions of 'democracy' the French Revolution of 1789 is an irrefutable historical monument. Since then, it can be said that three concepts of democracy have featured in European theoretical and political discourse, namely, 'liberal', 'social' and 'socialist' democracy. Theoretically, each emerged as a critique of pre-existing forms of rule and distribution of wealth. But after 1917 or the end of the First World War, politically all three coexisted, depending on the point of reference in Europe (including North America), e.g., Western Europe in general, Scandinavia in particular, and Eastern Europe. This produced three competing conceptions of democracy but two competing systems (not models) of political and economic organisation. It was the folly[1] of underdeveloped countries to construe these as models or abstracted forms freed of their substantive content.

It is important to warn that the term 'folly' is not used here to signify bad logic but rather political and social foolishness which itself is a product of what it responds to. For long periods ex-colonial countries saw themselves as extensions of metropolitan countries and often sought to reproduce the same models that had been imposed on them. This is common knowledge, and, to appreciate what it implies from the point of view of its historicity, we do not have to blame history on anybody. Our job is to decipher history as objectively as we can to be able to come to terms with ourselves as agents of history. The point is that ontological and ideological formulations arising out of given world-views and modes of thought will hold sway until they are questioned in practice.

In other words, any dramatic disintegration of historical models will be preceded by disillusionment or frustration in that society. In the process certain elementary and intuitive impulses will be transformed into fundamentally different perceptions and modes of thought which seek not merely to overthrow received models but, more specifically, to discredit the intellectual foundations upon which they rest. To prove the point, we can refer to the anti-colonial struggles in Africa. These are important historical antecedents which had been made by the people themselves through struggle.

As a consequence of their own actions, in rejecting one social order the protagonists have the obligation to produce an alternative— a world-view of promise and hope. Properly understood, this means that not only is there an intellectual dimension but also a utopian quality to any social negation. For instance, the notion of 'democracy' involves intellectual and political projections which transcend reality and by so doing it raises possibilities which are denied in present existence. It is our submission that it is precisely the discrepancy between what is experienced in real life and what is perceived as ideal life that is a source of tension in society and, therefore, a spring for revolutionary impulses. But, it should be noted that in no revolution is an ideal society realised or can be realised.

The theoretical implication of this observation is that utopia is a permanent feature of all social existence and a guarantee of incessant movement. The resounding slogan of the French Revolution, *'Liberté, Egalité et Fraternité'*, did not by any means result in equality and comradeship for the labouring classes, women and other disadvantaged persons. Its value lies in the fact that it burst asunder the boundaries of feudal society and inaugurated a new historical era wherein not only new freedoms could be enjoyed but also their limitations be recognised in practice. Like a counterpoint in music, here we experience two things at one and the same time, namely, qualitative change which is the essence of history and seeds for as yet an unknown and unknowable history, i.e., a new utopia. It transpires, therefore, that dynamically there is no way we can differentiate utopia and 'topia' (or status quo). They are constitutive elements of the same cycle and in their antithesis set the parameters within which actual social struggles or the making of history occur.

Democracy as Practice and Utopia

Anthropologically, it is probably true that the concept of 'democracy' is as old as humankind itself. What might have varied over time are its manifestations and conceptions. In this study it is its modern history that concerns us. As mentioned earlier, it can be asserted that in recent times three concepts of 'democracy' have emerged, accompanied by only two systems of political and economic organisation. These are all European in origin—something which Africans should never fail to remember, as our colonisers used to warn, but also something we can hardly fail to contemplate as the dawn of our own intellectual awakening approaches. As has already been acknowledged, the three concepts known to modern history are 'liberal', 'social' and 'socialist' democracy.

Their chronology is, of course, not as straightforward as their simple enumeration would suggest. Nonetheless, irrespective of whether one uses Cromwell's revolution in England or the French Revolution at its inception, 'liberal democracy' is by far the oldest. As a political form and a utopian vision, it pervaded Europe and its kindred extensions such as North America and the British dominions. For two hundred years it remained unrivalled. Therefore, not surprisingly, it is the best-studied and the most well-advertised form of 'democracy'. Its ideals, such as the freedom of speech, freedom of association, freedom of the press, rule of law and respect of individual rights, are still unexceptionable. Even the worst fascists in Europe and elsewhere swear by them to justify their social atrocities. Although at first sight this might strike us as a perversion or debasement of a concept, it could well be a sign of its atrophy at a particular historical juncture.

It is important to remember that all social concepts are historically determined. The alternative is to treat social concepts as absolute or transcendental. This would not be true of even religious dogmas. Otherwise, how else could we explain changes in religious beliefs and the emergence of new religions over time? Here, what it at stake is the question of transcendence, which implies supersession, atrophy or reinterpretation. This is what is understood by the diachronic approach. Its advantage is that, while it emphasises qualitative changes over time, it does not deny continuity. Thus within its terms of reference concepts can be treated relatively without denying their original authenticity. This is not to say that social concepts cannot be overthrown totally and cast into oblivion.

Theoretically and practically, liberal democracy reached its climax in the nineteenth century. Having presaged the rise of the second estate and the liberation of the third estate from serfdom in the eighteenth century, in the nineteenth it consolidated bourgeois power in production, science (particularly during the period 1834-65), and the arts (glorifying especially individualistic tendencies). It was the apogee of European ascendancy whose influence was felt far and wide. Under the ethos of liberal democracy 'enlightened' Europe reserved the right to subjugate and degrade less fortunate peoples (often referred to as 'savages') and even citizens.

We need not dwell on the perversions of liberal democracy in the colonies for that is intellectually 'boring' and often sounds life self-pity or a miserable attempt to find excuses for the feckless post-colonial rulers in the Third World. But stereotypes are also a way of telling unpleasant truths. They are unconvincing only because they are pre-coded messages for usually complex and changeable situations. Therefore, for the time being there is a strategic advantage in staying with the negations of liberal democracy at source, as depicted in extended analytical codes used by writers like Charles Dickens or Emile Zola in the middle and latter half of the nineteenth century.

It is possible that, from the point of view of social sciences, the studies by Engels or Sidney and Beatrice Webb on the conditions of the working class in nineteenth-century England would be the most appropriate references. But it is fair to acknowledge that, unlike the works of Dickens or Zola, these were not in the true liberal tradition. They were a critique which was aimed at undermining the social and theoretical foundations of liberal democracy on the basis of its negations, namely, class exploitation and domination.

These marked the beginnings of one of the three most intense political and intellectual movements in Europe since the industrial revolution. The issue was social democracy against liberal democracy. As is known, the inauguration of liberal democratic rights for all did not result in, and was not meant to, social equity for the workers in industrialised Europe. Some socialist, idealist and Marxist intellectuals tried to exploit this shortcoming and made it appear that 'the dictatorship of the proletariat' was within the reach of the workers. Events in 1848 proved otherwise. Everywhere the workers suffered a resounding defeat at the hands of their respective national bourgeoisie and military. This was to be expected because the European proletariat was still a fledging force, except perhaps in England, France and Germany. More importantly from our point of view, its leaders had been cast in the role of 'internationalists' by their political mentors before they had attained full command or mastery of their national situations at home.

This is in contrast to the bourgeoisie who were nationalists through and through and strove to consolidate their power nationally as a necessary condition for their imperialist ventures. Even at the international level the workers did not match the bourgeoisie. As yet there were very few labour unions or socialist organisations. It is not surprising, therefore, that when the First International or the International Workingmen's Association was projected in the 1860s, only a few and scattered groups were available. For this reason, and despite Marx's hopes, the First International was objectively a non-starter. In the end Engels had to admit in a letter to Sorge in 1874 that the First International was nothing else than a 'naive conjunction of all fractions'. But, like other socialist internationalists of his time, he failed to appreciate that social democracy was, and still is, an intrinsic part of the national question in Europe. The idea that socialism could develop outside the national question was erroneous, and was proven so by the scandalous capitulation by leading Western European social democrats on the eve of the First World War, as will be shown presently. Of course, recent events in Eastern Europe have repeated the capitulation, a subject which will also be commented upon.

The First International was a case of utopia gone wrong precisely because it tried to go beyond what was still in development in Europe, namely, the crystallisation of nation-states. It is interesting that its final collapse coincided with the unifications of Germany and of Italy— two countries which at the time had as many international socialists as any other in Europe. It was on the rock of nationalism in a double sense that 'international socialism' floundered. First, even the workers cherished the idea of belonging to a powerful nation-state, and those who were not in such a position were eagerly awaiting the day when they could. The latter was epitomised by what was called the Irish or Polish question and the right of self-determination among the Slavs and the Balkans— questions that have resurfaced with a vengeance and which have made the best European statesmen look like over-grown boys and the intellectuals tongue-tied. It is as if we are back in the times of the Second International.

As is well-known, the Second International was formed in 1889 to deal precisely with the question of social democracy and the right of nations to self-determination. In their essence these two themes revolved around the national question but, as happened then and in the present era of political duplicity and intellectual hypocrisy in Europe, they were subordinated to imperialism. This is a serious charge which any sincere European thinker cannot deny as a clear coincidence and which any serious African reformer or revolutionary (or a European one for that matter) can ignore only at their own peril. To support the case, we can refer to the struggle for social democracy in Europe and its abortion in the wake of European imperialist rivalries. Throughout Europe the struggle for social democracy was associated with the labour movement. In other words, it was workers' unions which gave birth to social democratic parties under the leadership of socialist intellectuals.

Though a latecomer in industrialisation, Germany produced the first union — German Workers' Unions in 1863; it was renamed the German Social-Democratic Workers' Party, and by 1911 it had become the biggest party in Germany. By then it lost its 'worker' appellation and known simply as the Social Democratic Party (SDP). It boasted some of the best political theoreticians in Europe between 1898 and 1914. These included such figures as Karl Kautsky (whom Engels in a moment of scepticism once referred to as 'the Pope of Socialism'), Edward Bernstein, Karl Liebknecht and Rosa Luxembourg — the Messiahs of international socialism, militantly anti-imperialist and anti-nationalist, who for this reason were sacrificed on the altar of German fascism. They were sacrificed with the complicity of their revisionist opponents within the Social Democratic Party. Unable to reconcile its commitment to 'international socialism' and defensive German nationalism, the party was forced to abandon its revolutionary path. It did so by becoming nationalistic to the point of being pro-imperialist, while it still favoured better wages for workers and greater political freedom at home. This is what came to be known as the *staatserhaltend* position — patriotic, liberal capitalist at home and imperialistic abroad.

This was the ultimate perversion of German social democracy. Obversely, it was the victory of revisionism, perhaps in circumstances which warranted it. The fact that towards the close of the nineteenth century leading social democrats could revert to Hegel's theory of 'historic' and 'non-historic' nations and no less a person than Bernstein could in defence of colonialism declare in writing in 1896 that 'to support savages and barbarians who resist the penetration of capitalist civilisation would be romantic' and that 'higher civilisations have rights superior to those of lower ones' (Davis 1976: 94-6). These views were fully condoned by Kautsky in his editorials in *Die Neue Zeit*. It is therefore not surprising that the SDP voted with the government for increasing the military budget in 1913, and in 1933 went so far as to endorse Hitler's aggressive policies only to be dissolved as a party by the same forces.

The history of social democracy in other leading European countries is no different. In England the movement first appeared as the Social Democratic Federation (SDF) in 1881. It was soon followed by the founding of the

Fabian Society in 1884. As in Germany, these groups represented left-wing intellectuals and worker-activists. Nonetheless, it was not until 1893 that the Independent Labour Party was formed, effectively under the leadership of the Trades Union Congress. It was the formation of the British Labour Party in 1906 that wrestled the leadership out of the hands of the workers and led to the incorporation of the social democratic movement into parliamentary politics. Already there had been a split in the movement during the Boer War between those who supported British imperialism in South Africa and those who saw the Boers as victims of an international capitalist conspiracy. In the name of social democracy nothing was said about the blacks who provided the labour and were being displaced from their lands precisely for this reason.

In contrast, the German revisionists found it convenient to reject 'patriarchal' exploitation in favour of 'capitalist' exploitation and to condone 'settlement colonisation' as against 'annexation of populated territories'. These are issues which might interest southern Africans at the present juncture, as their colonial past has become a factor in current debates about what is to be meant by 'social democracy' in their situations.

In England, as in Germany, the right wing of the social democratic movement abandoned the cause. Through organs such as the *British Citizen and Empire Worker* and *Blatchford's Clarion*, they, as C. F. Brand put it, 'turned a steady fire upon the left, and some of their staffs and correspondents surpassed the stoutest Tories in the violence of their attack'. Their jingoistic propaganda found great resonance in the hearts of the British workers who in the years leading up the First World War, as in Germany, voted for pro-imperialist policies. Unlike in Germany, however, all was not lost. The Fabian Society, despite its size and isolation from the workers, managed to introduce the principle of public utilities into Labour Party politics. Whether this could be spurned as 'sewer socialism', as did the disaffected social democrats, or accepted as a modicum of 'social democracy' in Britain is an open question. But there is no doubt that in order to gain parliamentary respectability the British Labour Party, like the German Social Democratic Party, had to pander to nationalistic and imperialistic sentiments in their fatherland.

This came as a bitter pill to the left-wing members of the movement. Somebody like James Connolly, who had high hopes for his colonised Ireland under would-be social democracy, could not help remarking ruefully that the British Labourites, 'like all apostates, are readiest to stab and destroy all those who remain true to that ideal of democratic freedom they have deserted and dishonoured' (Davis 1967: 126). It is interesting to note in this context that of all the Western European socialist or democratic parties, only the Irish, the Russian and Serbian parties—nationalities whose future is in the balance in the present ideological crisis in Europe—did not recapitulate in the period leading up to the First World War. The reason for their steadfastness was a combination of anti-imperialism and anti-capitalism, seen from the point of view of less developed nations in Europe. The analogy is too striking to be ignored by Third World meta-nationalists.

Suffice it to say, among other European countries with some degree of social democratic movement, it suffered the same fate as in Germany and England. In France, the home of European revolutions, the French Socialist Party, formed in 1895 was betrayed by its inability to deal with the national question. Although it enjoyed the support of the *Confédération Générale du Travail* (CGT) and fully recognised the bourgeois character of French democracy, it failed to elaborate a comprehensive national social democratic programme. Instead, it instilled the labouring class with an anti-nationalist and anti-patriotic spirit. This was a poor strategy, and on the eve of the First World War the proletariat internationalism of the CGT leaders and the rarified international socialism of the French Socialist Party evaporated like ether in the heat of nationalistic fervour among the rank and file. Pure Marxists such as Gustave Herve and Jules Guesde who formerly repudiated 'governmental and bourgeois patriotism' were forced to swallow their words and join the government. Those who, like Jean Jaures, refused to compromise became easy victims of the right wing just before actual hostilities broke out in 1914. Thus, as in Germany, no legacy of social democracy was left in France.

Italy is another European country which historically boasts a strong social democratic movement but not its successful fruition. Like in Germany, it became a victim of fascism during both world wars. Consequently, names of great Italian social democrats such as Andrea Costa, Filippo Turati—the editor of *Avanti*, Antonio Labriola, Gabriele D'Annunzio, Enrico Corradini, Angelo Olivetti, and, originally, Benito Mussolini are by now of only romantic interest. The likes of Mussolini, who as late as 1910 were breathing fire and brimstone against nationalism and imperialism and went so far as to tear up rail tracks to stop troops being sent to Libya, by the beginning of the First World War were ardent imperialists and fascists. They saw themselves as representatives of the 'proletarian nations' of Europe who had the national duty to break the monopoly of colonialism held by the 'plutocratic nations' of north-western Europe. All this had a sobering effect on future socialist leaders in Italy such as Antonio Gramsci, as will be seen later.

Indeed, the north-western Europeans had a great 'monopoly' regarding colonial empires, including small nations such as The Netherlands and Belgium. In Holland, where the social democratic movement was strongest, barring Germany, England and Ireland, there was a significant movement for the independence of Indonesia even during the war years. Their basic view was that imperialist wars were a burden not only on the colonised but also on the proletariat in the metropolitan countries. Opponents within the social democratic movement thought otherwise, maintaining that the industrialising countries needed colonies so as to improve the living standards of the working class in the 'civilised world'. This was consonant with the position of the majority of social democrats in the leading European countries on the eve of the First World War.

The Dutch Social Democratic Party, which became the Social Democratic Party in 1909, succeeded in defending social democracy at home and in maintaining its identity. By the time it gained parliamentary recognition as the Labour Party, these principles had already become part of Dutch political culture. This was a measure of the triumph of social democracy in Holland, unlike in other European countries where the social democratic movement flourished at all. It is important to note that the success of the Dutch social democratic movement is attributable to its becoming national rather than internationalist. All this did not augur well for the Second International which perforce disintegrated into national factions in 1914.

This collapse, however, by no means signalled the eclipse of social democracy universally. We have already referred to the Dutch case. In addition, there are the Scandinavian countries which in modern European history became the acknowledged symbols of social democracy. This is despite their not featuring in the great European social democratic movement, as epitomised by the First and Second Internationals. Unlike Holland, whose capitalist development predates the industrial revolution by far, modern Scandinavian capitalism does not date from earlier than the 1920s. Consequently, in the last half of the nineteenth century it was impossible for it to have produced a workers' social democratic movement. If so, can we then with impunity suggest that 'barbarians' stand to gain from the follies as well as the insights of their 'civilised' forerunners?

There appear to be no great theoreticians on the concept of social democracy in Scandinavia, as compared to other parts of Europe. In the absence of a workers' social democratic movement, social democracy in Scandinavia could only have come from above. Those responsible could only have benefited from the insights of especially the socialist 'revisionists' elsewhere in Europe prior to their scandalous recapitulation during the events leading up to 1914.

Whether or not Scandinavian intellectuals have reflected on this particular issue, it is worth noting that social democratic imposition might be part of their historical heritage. One has only to remember how Scandinavian monarchs long before the bourgeois revolution patronised peasants to defeat rebellious feudal lords. If the records be correct, then the Scandinavian peasants were not freed from bondage by a rising class, the bourgeoisie, but by an established traditional authority which had to pay a social price to continue to reign.

This might have been the precise position of the social democrats in Scandinavia (but not in Holland) since the second quarter of the present century. Currently, two contrary motions seem to be confronting them: first, under conditions which favour the right or the Christian Democrats, they are no longer prepared to pay the price in the same way that the socialist 'revisionists' did in the decade preceding the First World War; second, in the meantime the subordinate classes, sensing that all is not well with social democracy, are beginning to rebel against being patronised from above. Both actions sound the death-knell of Scandinavian social democracy and raise big questions about the future of social democracy universally.

The 'New Democracy'

After the collapse of the Second International and the elimination of socialist internationalists in Western Europe, the stage for socialist struggles moved to the East. This was a sequel to the first imperialist war (1914-18) and the first socialist revolution in Russia (1917). It was thought by socialists that these events marked the end of an epoch and the foreclosure of liberal democracy in imperialist-dominated countries. The underlying supposition was that, since liberal democracy was one of the achievements of a triumphant national bourgeoisie in leading capitalist countries in Europe, through imperialist imposition the same countries had now usurped the right of colonial and ex-colonial countries to produce their own autonomous national bourgeoisie. Not only this, the argument ran, but the imposition itself had in most cases inhibited the development of a national bourgeoisie because this had become a prerogative of the representatives of international capital. It was further supposed that under the circumstances the would-be national bourgeoisie in colonial and ex-colonial countries could at best play second fiddle to representatives of international capital in the imperialist countries. In other words, the rising petit-bourgeoisie in what is now known as the Third World could aspire only to a comprador status under capitalism.

It was in response to this scenario that the concept of the 'new democracy' was evolved and became the battle-cry of the Third International from 1919 onwards. As is known, its architects were the Russian socialists under the leadership of Lenin (the last of the German socialist militants, Rosa Luxembourg, having been assassinated the same year). But, ironically enough, it was not the Russians who succeeded in advancing the concept politically; rather, it was the Chinese under the leadership of Mao Tse-tung.

The causes of this development might be of great relevance in the present crisis of democracy in Eastern Europe and the Third World in general. Although it was agreed among socialist internationalists that under imperialism the petit-bourgeoisie in ex-colonial countries would be too feeble and compromised to guarantee national independence and popular democracy, and that it was the involvement of the workers and peasants in anti-colonial struggles which would prevent an outright political sell-out, the national question continued to be defined largely in class terms.

Over time there developed a disagreement on the issue. This centred on the role ascribed to each class. While all were agreed on the revolutionary role of the proletariat, there were reservations about the revolutionary capacity of two classes in particular, the peasants and the petit-bourgeoisie. As is known, Trotsky did not favour either class; in contrast, Lenin accorded a revolutionary role to the peasantry in colonial and ex-colonial countries. One class with which he would have no truck was petit-bourgeois nationalists, Lenin believing they would betray the workers and the peasants in the morrow of the revolution. This was consistent with his international socialist perspective. But, as the history of the Second International shows, such a philosophy failed to address the national question not only in colonial countries but also in colonising or imperialist countries.

After the death of Lenin, Stalin tried to solve this problem by recommending that the Third International should cooperate with petit-bourgeois nationalists in colonial countries so as to accelerate anti-colonial struggles. He therefore found it fitting to bring within the fold reactionaries such as Chiang Kai-shek who used the opportunity to get close enough to the Chinese Communist Party so as to destroy it from within. The scandalous betrayal of the Kuomintang is well-known. Its historical significance is that it exposed the inadequacies and dangers of the position of the European socialists and the limitations of their ill-defined concept of the 'new democracy'.

It is perhaps no accident that it was leaders such Mao Tse-tung and Ho Chi Minh from the colonised world who succeeded in situating the national question within their socialist trajectory. Their concept of the 'new democracy' cuts across classes, i.e., progressive and patriotic factions and strata from classes other than the peasantry and the workers qualified for membership in the democratic national alliance against colonialism and imperialism, provided their participation did not, in Mao Tse-tung's words, 'threaten the conditions of livelihood of the majority of the people'. By implication this excluded compradors and other blood-suckers (to use Marx's uncompromising language). It is, then, hardly surprising that these elements were driven out of the country both in China, as is shown by the ignominious retreat to Taiwan, and in Vietnam in the frenzied flight from Saigon after the American defeat.

This would clearly indicate that the 'new democracy' is anti-liberalism insofar as it has a definite idea of who its subjects and objects are. Indeed, Mao Tse-tung in his directive in September 1937 entitled 'Combat Liberalism' characterised liberalism as a licence for the petit-bourgeoisie to indulge itself and to dominate the conditions of livelihood of the majority of people in underdeveloped countries. In other words, under the concept of the 'new democracy' primacy is afforded to the 'conditions of livelihood of the majority of the people' and, while the national democratic alliance is given to all classes, it derives its national character from the fact that it is of necessity anti-imperialist.

This was an important departure from European socialist orthodoxy which predicated socialist democracy on international proletarianism and the dictatorship on the proletariat, both of which they failed to achieve. Instead, their movement floundered on the rock of nationalism and thus cleared the way for the ascendancy of the right-wing national bourgeoisie in Western Europe and the bureaucratic petit-bourgeoisie in Eastern Europe after the Second World War. The concept of the 'new democracy' tried to avoid these pitfalls by recognising the importance of national democracy and not just 'dictatorship' of the proletariat. It also aimed at forestalling petit-bourgeois excesses by emphasising the critical role of the workers and peasants in the struggle for national democracy whose objective was to guarantee the minimum 'conditions of livelihood' for the majority of the people.

For all its suppleness and originality, the concept did not meet with approval from the Third International under Stalin whose policies, at least in China, had given rise to its emergence in the first place. The Fourth International, under the influence of Trotsky, had rejected it outright. In subsequent debates on the transition to socialism in the West, which among others is typified by the sustained exchange between Paul Sweezy and Charles Bettelheim (1971), it received hardly any attention. It was not because it had failed in practice, as is shown by the historical victories in China, Cuba and Vietnam.

One suspects that part of the explanation is that the Northern socialists have always reserved the right to be scribes for the 'world revolution'. This suspicion is reflected in the writings of Southern writers such as Samir Amin. As is known, Amin vigorously defended the Maoist line as a response to what he perceived as European ethnocentrism even among the left in the West. He was particularly concerned about the role of nationalism in the Third World as a basis for anti-imperialist and anti-comprador struggles, trying to marry this with classical Marxist theory. The snag, however, is that classical Marxism has no theory of nationalism. This deprives Marxists of ready-made tools for dealing conceptually with the contradictions implicit in the articulation between national and class democracy or between Third World nationalism and socialism. It is important to recall that even the 'theory' of the right of nations to self-determination or Stalin's thesis on the national question left open the questions of under what conditions and what kind of national leadership.

The issue has now come back with a frightful vengeance in Eastern Europe and in Africa under the concept of 'democratic pluralism'. Those who saw possibilities in the Maoist position regarding anti-imperialist and national democracy are not able to reconcile this with the right of nations to self-determination, irrespective of the choices that are being made, e.g., in Eastern Europe. Involved here is the question of consolidation of fragmented social formations, especially in ex-colonial countries, and the future of socialism within the context of national democracy. There is a great tension between the two which has made it difficult for nationalistic Marxists such as Amin to develop a socialist critique of countries like China, Vietnam, Cambodia and Cuba within the context of national democracy.

The problem is compounded when we remember that Marxists of the same ilk have not decided whether capitalism is a necessary condition for socialist transformation. Suffice it to say, the concept of 'new democracy', as evolved by Mao Tse-tung, did not admit of 'capitalist roaders'. *In toto* it could be asserted that the 'new democracy' is neither liberal, social democratic in the sense of bourgeois social democrats in Europe, nor socialist in the sense of the European internationalist socialists who swore by the 'dictatorship of the proletariat' until their demise. It limited itself to two principles, national democracy and equity. While it cannot be affirmed theoretically whether this marks a transition to socialism or another development, these principles in their unity deserve our most serious attention.

The African Discourse

Against the background of the history of theories of democracy, there may be as yet no such a thing as 'African discourse' on democracy. Discourse is unrealisable without a set of conceptual tools derived from a coherent theoretical framework, whether proven or not. So far African intellectual debates on democracy have been eclectic, *ad hoc* (spontaneous) and empiricist in the sense that antagonists sought to validate their propositions by reference to single instances such as Kenya or Malawi. When these cannot suffice, recourse is made to more single instances which inevitably leads to arbitrary taxonomic classifications which have no theoretical value whatsoever. It is fair to point out that most of this is attributable to the adoption of American political science empiricist concepts and categorisation whose social and philosophical poverty is no recommendation to anybody.

The object of social science is not things but social phenomena in both their diachrony and synchrony. Therefore, there are no grounds why a phenomenon such as 'democracy' cannot be theorised on the basis of a systematic study of the social history of one country, say, Malawi or Kenya, in the same way that Lenin did in Russia or Mao Tse-tung in China. Both succeeded eminently in advancing knowledge and in evolving new political theories. In studying in detail the specific conditions in their respective countries, the intention was not to compare countries but to find historical grounds for pitting theory against theory. This is the true path to intellectual discovery and refutation. In the social sciences it is a guarantee for a socially and historically informed discourse, as against an argument about particular instances.

A debate on points can be exciting but it is not cumulative. Therefore, it is a poor basis for developing a discourse. In other words, it is impossible to generate meaningful sentences without any grammar. In the African academic debate on democracy since 1989 most protagonists failed to established the social and historical foundations of their object of discourse. 'Democracy' was treated as an item of vocabulary whose meaning depended on the user's intentions. For instance, the right to vote may or may not realise any democracy, subject to the actual content of social relations at a given historical juncture. Males have enjoyed the franchise in much of Europe for at least 150 years but in the process they realised more than one type of democracy. For example, it is apparent that liberal democracy has gradually waned since the First World War, so much so that since the Second World War Liberal parties have become minority parties. The big political battles have been fought between Labour/Social Democratic parties on the one hand and Conservative/Christian Democratic parties on the other.

Historically and substantively, liberal democracy has been superseded by other modes of bourgeois democracy. Liberalism was for all intents and purposes dead but for its letter. The term itself had become a swear-word both on the right and left of the contending forces. What has obscured the social and political significance of this is that the form it had inaugurated has remained. The rules of the game prevailed — call them parliamentary democracy and individual rights or 'human rights', to use the current jargon of the right in America and Europe. So, in insisting on liberal democracy, some African intellectuals can be accused of mistaking the form for its substance. If elsewhere the major battles are being fought between social democrats and representatives of monopoly capitalism personified by

Western leaders like Reagan, Thatcher, Bush and Kohl, how can they sound their clarion call for battle in such reactionary and antiquated terms?

Should not African intellectuals identify more clearly the contending social forces in their societies so as to be able to determine in a non-arbitrary fashion what kind of democracy is at issue on the continent? Analytically, it is not enough to make common-sense references to 'people' versus 'government' or to counterpose unconsciously 'civil society' versus 'government'. In the first instance, it is not sure what is meant by 'civil society', except that it has become fashionable among African scholars since the Atlanta seminar held to mark the inauguration of the Carter Centre at Emory University in February 1989. This was far from being an auspicious occasion. Mamdani said as much in his 'A glimpse at African Studies, Made in USA'. His scepticism went further, as is revealed by his reference to state versus society as a 'borrowed paradigm'. He might have been right in supposing that it was borrowed from Comparative Studies. This does not cut any ice as both are part of the same ahistorical empiricist tradition.

To grasp the full connotations of particular concepts, it behoves us to take cognisance of their social and historical origins. The term 'civil society' first appeared in modern European political vocabulary towards the end of the sixteenth century (c. 1592). This coincides with the final stages of the transition from feudal to bourgeois society in Europe. Unlike in feudal society where the dividing line was between free and bonded men, in the emerging bourgeois society the critical relationship was between 'state' authority and rights pertaining to 'citizenship' ('civil' in English and *civis* in French both derive from the Roman concept *civilis*, which drew a sharp distinction between 'citizens' and slaves/barbarians).

Of particular relevance to us is the fact that, after they had consolidated their power during the second half of the nineteenth century when there were increasing pressures from the working classes, as was shown, for installation of social democratic governments which were responsive to their demands, bourgeois theorists such as Auguste Comte in France and Herbert Spencer in England sought to forestall any intervention by the state by making it appear that there was an incompatibility between social legislation by the state and individual (bourgeois) rights. Is it not, therefore, an irony of history that we are now back to the social philosophies of the nineteenth century where the state was portrayed as the antithesis of 'civil society' rather than its product? Is it not a curious coincidence that in the midst of the World Bank/International Monetary Fund 'Structural Adjustment Policies' which betray great ambivalence towards the state in Africa that American political scientists are busy trying to find rationalisations for the same? Is this sufficient justification for African political scientists to have jumped on the bandwagon unreflectingly? What is their notion of 'civil society'—ethnic groups, non-governmental organisations or undifferentiated masses?

Putting aside the problem of fragmented social formations, at least in sub-Saharan Africa, it is well-known fact that 'people' in rural as well as urban Africa have become progressively differentiated into identifiable social classes or strata whose aspirations might predicate different types of 'democracy'. Therefore, while it might be logical to suppose that the 'government' represents identical interests, it is ahistorical to presume that any given populace within certain territorial borders necessarily constitutes a 'civil society'. If there had been in the historical sense civil societies, say, in sub-Saharan Africa (excluding Ethiopia), then the state would have been their direct product and become deeply entrenched in society. This would not imply absence of contradiction but would suggest that the state had no arbitrary or discretionary power. Rather, it is obliged by its own emergence to play the game according to the rules, whether these are subject to manipulation under the exigencies of given political struggles, e.g., the forced retreat of the working class after 1968 in Europe (the 'scotched hammer') or the precipitous collapse of 'socialism' in Eastern Europe (the return to a 'common European home').

In contrast, it can be asserted with confidence that the post-independence state in black Africa is a colonial product in a double sense. Not only is it an heir to the colonial state but also is a product of anti-colonialism which denotes a negative condition which brought together not so much an alliance of classes, as is popularly believed, but a coalition of different peoples. If it were to be argued that this coalesced into a civil society in the singular sense, then it would have to explained why even class politics in black Africa are still played in the idiom of ethnicity. The answer is that in most African states there is no unitary civil society. In many ways this vitiates the idea of a unitary state in Africa. By now, this is probably an incontestable proposition, if we were to think about it consistently.

Second, it is doubtful if it could be said with certainty that the anti-colonial or independence movement was at its inception and consummation a class alliance. The fact of the matter is that colonialism stunted the growth of classes in the capitalist sense in Africa, namely, representatives of capital and labour with the petit-bourgeoisie between as a service class. In the absence of any formed contending classes, the petit-bourgeoisie by virtue of its bureaucratic power, like the colonial government, usurped all the other classes in the process of developing. Not only this but in most cases it consolidated its political power without transforming itself into a national bourgeoisie.

This of itself thwarted further the development of what would be contending classes, perhaps not so much in the hinterland but more in the urban areas, where processes of industrialisation are crucial. Therefore, the suggestion that the independence movement was a class alliance might inadvertently attribute a greater class content to independence movements than actually existed. In turn, this would cast doubt on the validity of the thesis concerning the 'disintegration' of the class alliance of the independence movement. If this were the case it would be most felicitous, as it would imply that the contending classes had reached such a level of consciousness that they themselves would dictate the content of the new democracy.

Is this in fact the case? Are we able to infer from the current struggles in Africa the kind of democracy which is on the cards or are we simply projecting given images of democracy from abroad?

If we were to admit that there has never been a national democratic alliance in ex-colonial Africa, what would be the theoretical implications for us? Could we, for instance, view what is happening in Ethiopia, Eritrea, Tanzania, Zambia, Benin, Zaire, Kenya, Togo, Nigeria, etc., as a new alliance of classes which foreshadows the advent of a new democracy or a repetition of what petit-bourgeois nationalists had implemented in Africa after independence? In other words, would not there be any difference between simply a change of personnel and an attempt to inaugurate a true national democratic alliance?

Even in ancient Ethiopia the existence of a multiplicity of civil societies makes this question difficult to answer without checking the actual content of the present political struggles there. But at least in this part of Africa the issues are posed very sharply, unlike elsewhere where there is undoubtedly a return to liberalism and recapitulation as a response to the new Western right-wing ideological offensive called 'multi-party democracy' and 'respect for human rights'. Those who are interested in form rather substance might have problems in deciding whether this makes any difference whatsoever to what is cynically referred to as the 'people'. The cynicism lies in the fact that all along the 'people' in the Third World have not been able to win genuine democracy for themselves because Western powers have consistently aided and abetted their enemies.

In Africa easy reference could be made to the role of the Americans and the British in southern Africa, to the unwavering support they gave to Mobutu in the Congo and to various Kenyan regimes, both of which are now being sacrificed because they have become a political liability in the new battle for the hearts and the minds of the people of the Third and the Second World (Eastern Europe). The people who have been hankering after democracy all these years take this as genuine. Hence they vote for it, including the trade unions. But how tangible will be the results in either the Third or the Second World? This brings to the fore the question of what is the content of the new Western-sponsored 'democracy' in Africa and elsewhere? This question is barely touched on by African intellectuals, except by way of liberal incantations or effusions of fancy.

In the current debate on democracy in Africa it is probably accurate to say that it was Peter Anyang' Nyong'o who fired the first salvos (1987). According to our reading, his two related theses which were reiterated in his subsequent writings (1989) and polemics with Thandika Mkandawire (1989), are: first, the disintegration of the national alliance that led to independence ushered a phase of dictatorships in Africa (personal dictatorships even at that); and, second, the resultant lack of democracy in Africa is the root-cause of lack of development, i.e., there can be no development in Africa without democracy.

On the first thesis, as has already been pointed out, Anyang' has first to prove that there were formed classes prior to independence in Africa and that they were allied before he can postulate their disintegration. In doing so he might throw light on the question of what national democratic alliances can be expected in the course of the present upheavals in Africa. What would be their social basis and content, as against what happened at independence?

Anyang's second thesis is easily controvertible, as Mkandawire (1989) has not failed to point out. Germany and Japan and lately Taiwan and South Korea are most eminent examples of where development occurred without democracy in any of the three senses in which it has been used in this paper. Second, in what strikes one as a vain attempt, Anyang' tried to prove his case by offering Kenya and Cote d'Ivoire as two countries in Africa which achieved development precisely because they maintained some modicum of democracy. Both suppositions are extremely dubious, unless we are guided by the standards of the World Bank and the IMF. Further proof of Anyang's folly was the fact that he could not fit Malawi, Banda's fiefdom, into his scheme of things.

Finally, Anyang' fell a victim of the worst kind of empiricism when he tried to classify African countries according to whether they were 'repressive' or 'more liberal'. This is theoretically inadmissible because democracy cannot be treated as a divisible quantum of which we can have more or less. Rather, it is an enduring state of society, though it be subject to the usual strains and stresses of social existence. Thatcher, Reagan and Bush, the three Western leaders who did most to dispense with liberal and social democratic remnants in bourgeois democracy, dare to speak loudest about the preservation of 'Western democracy'. It is all not a lie, despite the political vicissitudes of individual Western capitalist countries, especially the former Mediterranean dictatorships and former champions of fascism such as Germany (something which is still lurking in the background).

Concerning Africa, the question that has to be seriously considered is whether or not since independence there has ever been an enduring state of society which could reasonably be described as 'democracy', instead of making inconsequential distinctions between autocratic regimes and rules by capricious 'presidents for life'. It cannot be said too often that the issue here is not personal concessions from what Anyang', ironically enough, calls 'benevolent dictators' or Samir Amin (1990) more accurately characterises as 'petty democracy' but the enduring state of society. Are we able to affirm, without ambiguity, that Anyang's 'more liberal' regimes in Africa are in this regard different in type? If so, what type of democracy do they represent and how was it socially evolved, noting that any regime can go through the variations postulated by Anyang' without changing its social character?

Anyang' had been accused of 'instrumentalism' by Mkandawire (1989) in positing that democracy was a necessary condition for development. Although the converse of Anyang's postulate, namely, that a continuing crisis of accumulation is almost impossible to combine with expansion of democracy (Mafeje 1975; Amin 1990) is sustainable, this does not mean that one is the function of the other. It only draws attention to an important inequation which, for instance, sets a limit to the development of social democracy in underdeveloped countries even under populist regimes and casts doubt on the viability of the new imperialist-sponsored 'democratic pluralism' in Africa and elsewhere.

All this does not necessarily exonerate Anyang' from Mkandawire's charge, nor does it explain it. A careful deciphering of Anyang's texts would reveal that when he takes leave of the neo-Marxist lexicon he lapses into the instrumentalism of American political science to which he is no stranger since his Chicago days. The latter might be incidental but what matters, theoretically, is that largely unknown to itself (a notable exception being David Apter (1961) who made explicit his philosophical foundations by using the binary opposition between 'consummatory' and 'instrumental' values; this is also implicit in Goran Hyden's concept of 'economy of affection'), American political science was heavily influenced by John Dewey's instrumentalist philosophy which made a radical distinction between 'ceremonial' and 'instrumental' behaviour (Dewey 1929). It was the latter which was associated with the development of the West.

This is certainly not what Mkandawire had in mind when he made his charge and in all probability Anyang' never intended it, but his presuppositions and lexicon betray an identifiable intellectual reflex whose philosophical connotations might prove incompatible. Perhaps, it is this which Mkandawire should have fastened on, seeing that he swears by Gramsci in these matters. One suspects, though, that Mkandawire quoted Gramsci in vain and in so doing might have succeeded more in 'disturbing' Anyang' than in convincing him. Gramsci's injunctions are intelligible only if subordinated to the political conceptions he was actively evolving in reaction to existing Marxist orthodoxies of the Second International. Also, as an Italian, he was concerned to break with the culturalist/idealist tradition of Croce, under whose weight most Italian intellectuals laboured. To this end Gramsci introduced certain key concepts, among which 'hegemony', 'civil society' and 'organic intellectuals' gained lasting ascendancy. In addition, instead of thinking of Marxism as a 'theory without a subject', he saw it as a 'philosophy of praxis', as is shown by his dictum: 'The advancing man (not to offend feminist sensibilities) always triumphs in the end'. It is, perhaps, this attitude of mind which attracts Mkandawire.

Contrary to Anyang's and Mandaza's suspicion, it did not in any way imply idealism but irrevocable commitment to struggle. What might detract from Mkandawire's case is the fact that after assuring all concerned that 'democracy' was an absolute value (i.e., a value in itself), he relativised his position by crediting 'liberal democracy' as better than nothing—a position which was surprisingly endorsed by Gutto (1990) as well as Mamdani (as quoted by Shivji 1990). In Gramsci's problematique none of this would arise. Under his concept of 'hegemony' social rights are neither assumed nor given but belong to a contested terrain between the state and civil society, conceived as an 'ensemble of private interests' located somewhere (albeit vaguely) between the 'economic structure' and the 'superstructure' (public life and the state). 'Hegemony' is given neither to the state nor to the official parties but to those social alliances which enjoy the greatest ideological resonance in society at a given time (e.g., the Catholic Church in Italy in Gramsci's time). This leads directly to the concept of 'organic intellectuals' for this is the social milieu in which they realise themselves as a political and ideological force.

Therefore, it would seem prejudical and anachronistic to talk of 'liberal democracy', as if it were a natural starting-point or the nearest thing to attain in Africa. What the struggles for democratic rights in Africa will usher in, as elsewhere, will depend on which social alliances will become hegemonic in society. An analysis of the balance of forces in Africa at the present historical juncture should at least give us some indication, instead of being guided purely by our wishes or intellectual prejudices. Of course, our social projections, as organic intellectuals, matter and are necessary.

From the point of view of 'philosophy of praxis', there is always an underlying tension between determinism and voluntarism. Intended or not, this manifested itself in the exchange between Shivji and Mandaza (1990). Mandaza was inclined to accuse Shivji of determinism or 'waiting for Godot' in his academic and theoretical tower (unkind words, perhaps communicated as a sign of respect and appreciation), while not only reserving the latter for himself but advocating it for others on the basis of his experience in Zimbabwe, without acknowledging that it is a mixed one. He also chastised Shivji for 'caricaturism'. Perhaps Shivji deserves what he got. He trivialised his own problematique by presenting it in a Charlie Chaplin fashion. (One wonders why but also one recalls that in his prison notes Gramsci affected certain verbal postures; so it could be with anybody.) But, as is known, Charlie Chaplin's message was always very profound, to the disquiet of the Americans who found it necessary to deport him back to his native England.

Irrespective of the reaction, Shivji elicited from his colleagues (irritation from Mandaza and disgust from Anyang' if only with his 'hackneyed terms'), his diagnosis is more correct than most and, theoretically, is better founded than that of his detractors. For instance, on liberalism and imperialism or 'fashionable bandwagons' of the West, his observations are valid and Mandaza could not help granting this. His concept of 'compradorial democracy' might be etymologically vulgar and theoretically undeveloped but, as a shorthand for what is happening or likely to happen in Africa under the current *pax Americana*, it hits the nail on the head.

All evidence points to the fact that in the so-called 'wave of democratisation' sweeping through Africa a new class of compradors will gain ascendancy. They will be largely technocrats who will try their best to ingratiate themselves with the World Bank and to give its Structural Adjustment Programmes in Africa a longer lease of life. Unlike their predecessors, they will be less nationalistic, more pro-West and will espouse some naive and anachronistic ideas about liberal democracy. In the hope of achieving the long-awaited democracy since independence, the people will vote for them as before. But disillusionment will come fast.

It is not so much that one bears the new compradors malice but that, far from being a solution to the African problem, they are themselves an aberration. It is already apparent that the Structural Adjustment Programmes are no cure for the continuing economic malaise in Africa and that Western countries are not about to make any more financial concessions to Africa for good political reasons. When it comes to content, the new compradors will have no more to offer than their discredited predecessors. Irrespective of their level of consciousness, people do not vote without expectations. Their subjective interest at all times is to reproduce themselves socially. If so, what can the new compradors offer them socially? Austerity measures under IMF 'conditionality'?

This aside, it is worth noting that under the present conditions in Africa 'incrementalist' democracy has led to disillusionment rather than optimism among the rank and file. Recent examples such as Zimbabwe, Namibia, Lesotho under the King, post-Nyerere Tanzania and, predictably, Zambia are good barometers for measuring what is in store for the rest. In spite of the current wave of liberalism, disillusionment is not necessarily a bad thing, as it forces people to look elsewhere for genuine solutions. Given the existing negations, genuine democracy is not so difficult to define, if still difficult to achieve. Although revolutionaries are often obsessed with 'state power', it is apparent that not only is the *demos* destined never to exercise something called 'state power', nor are ordinary people interested in such an abstraction, except insofar as it affects their chances of livelihood. Indeed, it is a matter of common observation that, although it does not always happen, ordinary people only fight when their livelihood is threatened. In other words, they fight in order to guarantee the necessary conditions for their social reproduction.

Regarding present conditions in Africa, this can refer only to two things: first, the extent to which the people's will enters decisions which affect their life chances; and, second, the extent to which their means of livelihood are guaranteed. In political terms the first demand does not suggest capture of 'state power' by the people (workers and peasants) but it does imply ascendancy to state power by a national democratic alliance in which the popular classes hold the balance of power. The second demand implies equitable (not equal) distribution of resources. Neither liberal democracy, imposed 'multi-partyism' nor 'market forces' can guarantee these two conditions. It transpires, therefore, that the issue is neither liberal nor 'compradorial' democracy but social democracy. It is a happy coincidence that this has become an issue everywhere in the world, including Western Europe at a time when it is proposing to rescue Eastern Europeans from socialist dictatorships. In reality, what is it going to be: a recolonisation of the Third and the Second Worlds by Western imperialism or are the barbarians once again poised to liberate the 'civilised' (remember the Roman Empire and the colonial empires) by liberating themselves?

In the African context one would have liked to refer to Uganda, Eritrea and even Ethiopia after Mengistu, but that would probably be premature. But it is worth noting that this is just a beginning. The new compradors are in all probability matched by a new breed of African meta-nationalists who are strongly anti-imperialist and regionalist in outlook and committed to the principle of social equity for their own survival and that of their countries in the intermediate and long term. For the time being, they are disadvantaged because they have neither state power, sufficient financial means, nor the people behind them. This is so either because social disillusionment is not yet deep enough or because their own impact as organic intellectuals is not yet felt — something which is not entirely sure, judging by the responses of the various African regimes.

In conclusion, it can be said that as yet there is no African discourse on democracy because African intellectuals have on the whole responded to disparate aspects of the problem, without consciously trying to find studied terms of reference which would enable them, even in disagreement, to develop a totalising critique. For instance, Shivji and Gutto, given a rich history of jurisprudence, should have been able to provide a learned political economy of the ideas surrounding the various concepts of 'democracy' and thus make apparent logical possibilities under the present conditions in Africa.

African political scientists, brought up in the self-unaware American instrumentalist philosophy, were not the best placed to contribute to a philosophically and theoretically profound critique of the prevailing concepts of democracy in Africa. Although in the current debate African scholars gave a lot of space to it, they have been handicapped by its ahistoricism and frustrated especially by its social philosophical poverty. It has to be admitted in all honesty that American political science propositions are both vulgar and inane. If African scholars were to abandon them *in toto*, instead of screaming and shrieking about them, they would not get any poorer by it but might, conceivably, gain for themselves the necessary space for original and creative thinking.

This is no mere rejection of Western forms of knowledge. As regards issues such as 'democracy', we still have such worthy disciplines as philosophy, jurisprudence, history and classical sociology. However, it has to be recognised that the disciplines themselves do not matter; what matters is their contribution to our understanding of current issues both in their local and universal perspective.

Note
1. The term 'folly' does not mean here 'illogical' but 'silliness' a social and political silliness which in itself is a product of what it corresponds to.

References

Amin, Samir, 1990, 'The issue of Democracy in the Contemporary Third World', CODESRIA Symposium, 26-29 November, Kampala, Uganda.

Anyang' Nyong'o, Peter (ed.), 1987, *Popular Struggle for Democracy in Africa*, Zed Books, London.

------------, 1988, 'Political Instability and Prospects for Democracy in Africa', *Africa Development*, XIII, 1: 71-86.

------------, 1989, 'A Rejoinder to the Comments on Democracy and Political Instability, *CODESRIA Bulletin*, I:13-14.

------------, 1990, 'Democracy and the Economy', *SAPEM*, 3, 4, February.

------------, 1991, 'Development and Democracy: The Debate Continues', *CODESRIA Bulletin*, 2:2-4.

Apter, D, 1961, *The political Kingdom in Uganda*, Princeton University Press, Princeton.

Davis, H, B, 1967, *Nationalism and Socialism: Marxist and Labour Theories of Nationalism to 1917,* Monthly Review Press, NY.

Dewey, J, 1929, *Quest for Certainty*, New York.

Fozzolini, A, *Antonio Gramsci: An introduction to His Thought*

Gramsci, A, 1971, *Selections from the Prison Notebooks*, edited by H, and N, Smith, Lawrence and Wishart, London.

Gutto, S, B, O, 1990, 'The Way Forward: Sustainable Development and People's Democracies in Africa', *SAPEM*, 3,11 September.

Mafeje, A, 1976, 'State Capitalism in Predominantly Agrarian Societies', in *Ideology, Science and Development,* Scandinavian Institute of African Studies, Uppsala.

Mandaza, Ibbo, 1990, 'Democracy in the African Reality', *SAPEM*, 11, September.

Mao Tse-Tung, 1967, *Selected Works*, Vol. II, Foreign Language Press, Pekin, 339-384.

Mkandawire, T, 1989, 'Comments on Democracy and Political Instability', *CODESRIA Bulletin*, I, pp.11-12.

------------, 1991, 'Further Comments on the Development and Democracy Debate', *CODESRIA Bulletin*, 2:11-12.

Shivji, Issa, 1990, 'Pitfalls of the Debate on Democracy', *SAPEM*, 3, 4 February.

Sweezy, P, M, and Bettelheim, C, 1971, 'On the Transition to Socialism', *Monthly Review Press*, NY.

3. Discourses on Democracy in Africa

Peter Anyang' Nyong'o

Introduction

I call on all ministers, assistant ministers and every other person to sing like parrots. During Mzee Kenyatta's period, I persistently sang the Kenyatta tune until some people said: 'This fellow has nothing to say except to sing for Kenyatta'. Therefore you ought to sing the song I sing. If I put a full stop you should put a full stop. This is how the country will move forward.

Daniel Toroitich Arap Moi, Kenyan President

Daily Nation, 14 September 1984

Surely a notion of modern government in Africa in such terms as given in the quotation above cannot even be a pale shadow of democracy as it has been conceived of down the ages and across cultures. Kamuzu Banda once described himself as a 'dictator that the people choose to put up with' (Short 1974). At least here there is a mention of the people making a choice about who governs them. The truth, however, is that they do not make that choice under an authoritarian presidency, although they may choose to put up with it in various ways. And democracy is not only about the governed choosing their governors; they must do more than that, and control them—and this is where the tenets of democracy become universal.

This universality was present in the independence constitutions of African states but was soon denied by the nationalists as they consolidated themselves in political power. Rupert Emerson (1960:272-92) was probably right when he predicted, as early as 1960, that democracy in Africa, as in Asia, would bleed and die on the altars of national consolidation and social reconstruction. History has vindicated Professor Emerson, but with the social tragedy the African nations have not been consolidated nor have societies been reconstructed in a positive way, i.e., to improve the lot of the African people (Anyang' Nyong'o 1991). Why has Africa trodden this rather tragic path in her post-independence history? What happened to the inspiring and heroic democratic struggles that the nationalists waged?

This paper seeks to trace the discourses on democracy in Africa from the days of African nationalism to the present. It is argued that one of the most inspiring ideals of the independence movement was democracy. Around the call to establish a democratic society hinged other issues of interest to diverse sections of the African people mobilised in support of the nationalist political agenda. This agenda, though strong in its appeal and capable of mobilising social movements which forced the change in the political character of society and ushered in majority rule, rarely envisaged the continued political mobilisation of the people in the post-independence era. In actual fact, political mobilisation and popular participation in politics soon became anathema to the task of nation-building (Huntington 1968).

Limited notions of democracy thus started to appear, and these proved to be more of rationalisations of various forms of presidential authoritarianism than really innovative and alternative theoretical discourses on democracy (e.g., Sklar 1982). In this genre was the argument for 'one-party democracy', an argument first powerfully advanced by Nkrumah (1957), followed by Nyerere (1963), Sékou Toure, Tom Mboya (1963) and then, as if it had become the credential for passing as a Pan-Africanist, by all other leaders who declared one-party rule in their states.

It would, perhaps, be historically incorrect to argue that the first advocates of 'one-party democracy' had, from the very beginning, a hidden agenda of authoritarianism. Authoritarianism arguably emerged historically: as the post-colonial state was faced with competing demands for scarce resources, only those which could be processed into outputs without disrupting the system were allowed in through the political sluice-gates of authoritarian governance. This would be Huntington's argument, an argument we will need to delve into below, with the benefit of hindsight.

Intense struggles have, however, continued to put the case for democracy and to challenge the authoritarian presidential political systems. Sometimes these struggles have led to searches for quick solutions, i.e., through military coups or putsches (Decalo 1986). At other times they have appeared in the form of what one might call romantic revolutions. Being disillusioned with the non-democratic and authoritarian presidential states, revolutionary intellectuals found Marxism very appealing, and possibilities of bringing about social justice through socialist revolutions led to the Marxist intelligentsia supporting various shades of revolutionary regimes (at times called 'Afro-Marxist' regimes) as popular democracies: So-called 'socialist revolutions' — in Guinea, Mozambique and Angola — have been nothing but disasters. We prefer calling them 'romantic revolutions' rather than 'socialist' so as not to continue giving a bad name to socialism.

In the midst of all this, the real nature of popular struggles for democracy in Africa was rarely understood, let alone studied. For, under authoritarian regimes, it was not easy to mobilise the people to assert their democratic rights and defend themselves against authoritarianism. This struggle took place in many forms, in guises if you will, but it was there nonetheless, and it eventually started to bear fruit when the international context of African politics changed towards the end of the 1980s. We were the first to take a careful look into these popular struggles and 'their various guises' (Anyang' Nyong'o 1987), at a time when discussions on democracy in Africa, apart from the systematic studies of Richard Sklar, were not in vogue.

In other words, Africa has had a heritage of democratic struggles, and this heritage has its own internal discourse(s). Both the heritage and the discourse need to be studied in a well-understood historical context. Hence our interest in writing on this subject is not to prove the existence of an African variant of democracy. C. B. Macpherson (1973) attempted this, and concluded that the Africans belonged to the 'non-liberal democracy': the underdeveloped variant, and ended up by making a case for what later became known as 'developmental authoritarianism'. By contrast, we wish to see how an important political ideal (democracy) has been discussed in Africa, what its bearing has been on political praxis and its place in the processes of social transformation.

Democracy and the Nationalists

In order not to make history look too simple, and indeed to avoid the great danger of over-generalisation, we shall not venture into discussing African nationalism before the Second World War. After 1945 there began to emerge some common patterns of political development, especially with regard to the movement for independence and its demands (or political agenda). This can perhaps be traced to the Pan-Africanist movement that Nkrumah and others started in London (Nkrumah 1957), and the ideals for the liberation of the African people they started to share, as for example in the Declaration of the All African People's Conference held in Accra, Ghana, in 1958. In this regard, the independence of Ghana in 1957, and the precedent it set, cannot be minimised.

The main focus on independence, and what it would mean in the rest of Africa (constitutional government of the Westminster type— and even the one-party system) came from 1957 onwards. As Tom Mboya (1963) noted:

> Before Ghana there were only Egypt, Liberia, Sudan and Ethiopia as independent states, and their history was so different they did not have a similar impact on post-war nationalist aspirations in the rest of Africa. The first conference of Independent African States was held in Accra in April 1958, and it passed resolutions which highlighted the struggle for independence.

This conference was soon followed, in December of the same year, by the All African People's Conference, which Nkrumah described as having brought together freedom fighters from all over the continent to wage a final assault on imperialism and the complete eradication of colonialism from the continent.[1] All told, there were 300 delegates representing the entire continent of Africa, and a good number of these were soon to be presidents (like Nyerere), prime ministers (like Lumumba) and key ministers in their respective governments (like Mboya).

The conference, as it were, focused on galvanising an African anti-imperialist front and giving courage to all those still under colonial domination to fight for independence under a pan-Africanist banner. The only time the conference discussed democratic principles was with reference to independence *per se* and the right of all colonised peoples to self-determination. In its Declaration to the Colonial People of the World, drawn up by Nkrumah, the conference asserted:

> We believe in the rights of all peoples to govern themselves. We affirm the right of all colonial peoples to control their own destiny. All colonies must be free from foreign imperialist control, whether political or economic. The peoples of the colonies have the right to elect their own government, a government without restrictions from a foreign power. We say to the peoples of the colonies that they must strive for these ends by all means at their disposal ... the struggle for political power by colonial and subject peoples is the first step towards, and the necessary prerequisite to, complete social, economic and political emancipation (Anon 1973:82).

This, for its time, was a very far-reaching declaration. Indeed, the very idea that Africans could think of ruling themselves, in other words of enjoying the very first steps towards self-determination, was an important step in liberating the colonised psyche. Second was the need to make the African peoples aware that, however paternalistic and benevolent colonial rule was, it could not be a substitute for the emancipation that would come with independence. The very idea of being free of foreign political, economic, cultural and ideological domination was good in and of itself. All other things would subsequently follow, and this included democratic governance.

These other things could not be achieved unless the Africans, in their struggle for independence, submerged their differences and fought in unity. This unity made mobilisation for achieving the single goal of independence, 'Uhuru' or 'Kwacha' easy, since the enemy (the colonial power) is then targeted by all social forces within the independence movement, not party. As Mboya (1963: 61-2) put it:

> In this way one word summarises for everyone the meaning of the struggle, and within this broad meaning everyone has his own interpretation of what Uhuru will bring to him. The simple peasant may think of Uhuru in terms of farm credits, more food, schools for his children. The office clerk may see it as meaning promotion to an executive job. The apprentice may interpret it as a chance to qualify as a technician, the schoolboy as a chance for a scholarship overseas, the sick person as the provision of better hospital facilities, the aged worker as the hope of pensions and security in old age.

The interpretation of the goal is not immediately relevant or important, when compared with the importance of mobilisation of the entire population ... The people have to be organised so that they are like an army: they must have a general, they must have discipline, they must have a symbol. In many cases the symbol is the national leader himself, and it is necessary to have this kind of symbol of an heroic father-figure if you are to have unquestioning discipline among the different groups and personalities who should rally their followers behind him.

Much later in the essay, Mboya (1963:87) realises that the diverse expectations of the outcome of independence by the members of the movement (or the nationalist coalition) may degenerate into disunity and conflicts soon after independence, making it difficult to hold the ship of state on course in pursuit of economic reconstruction and development. An argument is therefore advanced for the single-party system headed by a strong national leader, not only to safeguard unity in the face of adverse threats to independence (East-West rivalries, personality clashes, etc.) but also to ascertain the discipline necessary for rapid development.

This is much more so since, as Nyerere (1968) argues elsewhere, the African people are generally agreed on what they need after independence: development. Not divided into different social classes that warrant representation under different political parties with competing ideologies and world views, the single-party system becomes more or less a natural framework for organising democratic government in Africa.

Mboya (1963:89) asserts:

The safeguards for democracy in Africa lie elsewhere. They rest upon the integrity of leaders, who have enormous power for good or evil because of the confidence the masses place in them. The risk that a leader may do great evil before he is challenged is the biggest risk democracy faces, but it is a risk these states must logically and inevitably take if they are to face the challenges of independence... Another safeguard lies in the proper working of the party machinery, which should ensure the opportunity for full and frank discussions, so that decisions are taken democratically.

Oginga Odinga (1967:23) carried this need for discussion and participation some steps further:

But a one-partly government could be democratic only if the mass of the people were associated with policy-making at all levels, if the people were drawn into the running of the party, if national issues were discussed in the branches, at public meetings, at conferences, in our newspapers, among the women and the youth; if careful thought was given to the role of the party in relation to the administration so that civil servants trained in the pre-colonial attitudes could not, in the day-to-day running of the country, undo the best plans made by the political leadership.

And, one could add, for the leaders to maintain integrity and the party to ensure full and frank discussions. Mboya (1963) advocated the unfettered safeguard of fundamental human rights in independent Africa. Basic freedoms had to be ensured, the sanctity of human life prescribed and the rule of law accepted as an important pillar of independence.

When Mwalimu Julius Nyerere appointed a Presidential Commission on the Establishment of a Democratic One Party State in Tanganyika in 1964, he stated part of the task of the commission as follows:

> Specifically, I have instructed the Commissioners, in their consideration and examination, to observe the principles that:
>
> (a) Tanganyika shall remain a Republic with an executive Head of State:
>
> (b) The Rule of Law and Independence of the Judiciary shall be preserved;
>
> (c) There shall be complete equality of all Tanganyika citizens;
>
> (d) There shall be the maximum political freedom for all citizens within the context of a single national movement;
>
> (e) There shall be the maximum possible participation by the people in their own government and ultimate control by them over all the organs of the State on a basis of universal suffrage;
>
> (f) There shall be complete freedom of the people to choose their own representatives on all Representative and Legislative bodies, within the context of the law (Cliffe 1967:438-9).

Given these basic democratic concerns, Nyerere wanted the commission to advise on how they could be realised and sustained in a one-party system. He added: 'I think I should emphasise that it is not the task of the Commission to consider whether Tanganyika should be a One Party State. That decision has already been taken'.

A case could have been put, however, to the extent that the one-party system, by its very nature, especially under conditions of underdevelopment, necessarily gravitates towards authoritarianism. But not at that point in time, for Nyerere himself (1963) had eloquently dismissed multi-party systems as 'football democracies', and students of Tanzanian politics, writing furiously on 'one-party democracy' in Tanzania, heavily focused on electoral participation as a significant index of a working democracy (e.g., Cliffe 1967). But could things have been otherwise in the mid-1960s?

The confidence with which the nationalists ruled, the power that the masses still had within their organisations as component parts of the nationalist coalition, and the relative expansiveness of the national cake made democracy within the one-party state a lived experience. But it did not take long before the contradictions that Mboya feared would put a strain on the unity of the nationalist coalition started to challenge the democratic character of the one-party system.

Jaramogi Oginga Odinga (1967:284) has summarised these contradictions, which led him and others to break away from the coalition and form an opposition party, in the following terms:

> The party, as the expression of the will of the ordinary people, was not being allowed to function, and despite repeated requests by branches for the holding of a conference and new elections, head office stalled on this demand.
>
> Leaders in government and party were retreating from the people, that every excuse was being made to avoid consulting them, and that government by a small circle of leaders could too easily be influenced by forces against the national interest.
>
> Political intrigue, caucus decisions and ambitions for office cannot thrive side by side with a vigorous, popularity-based party machine, or democratic decision-making of any kind.

Finally, Odinga asserted, unity could only be maintained if people discussed and agreed on policies, if such policies were really in the interest of the members of the coalition. As it turned out, not only had discussion been diminished, but policies were being pursued against the interest of the coalition members in the areas of employment, economic development, foreign affairs, agriculture, class privileges and the distribution of political power.[2]

The assumption that the one-party state represented everybody and sought to promote their general interest was torpedoed by an essay by Issa Shivji (1970) with reference to Tanzania. It became a classic of the leftist critique of the single-party system and its ideological rationalisation, African socialism — about which Ahmed Mohiddin (n. d.) had already pronounced a radical indictment as being 'neither African nor socialist'.

For the state to represent everybody and to serve everybody's interests, it had not only to get rid of the colonial iniquities against which independence struggles were fought, but it had also to 'deliver the goods' of social justice and equality. But the practices of African socialism — Africanisation and nationalisation — did not really lead to the masses doing better than before or their feeling they were now in control. These two programmes were rapidly producing a new breed among African society, particularly among the nationalist political entrepreneurs: the 'nizers' (Shivji 1970) or those who had 'fallen into things'. And since they did not want everybody to fall into these things — the things were few (economics of scarcity) — they logically used the power they had in political control (the state) to control access to these things, i.e., to determine the structure of opportunity.

Okot p'Bitek (1989:110) put it even more vividly:
And those who have
Fallen into things
  Throw themselves into soft beds,
  But the hip bones of the voters
  Grow painful
  Sleeping on the same earth
  They slept
Before Uhuru!
  And they cover the ulcers
On their legs
With animal skins.

And when they have
Fallen into things
They become rare,
Like the python
With a bull water buck
  In its tummy.
They hibernate and stay away
  And eat!

Thus, when political scientists were busy studying political parties in the late 1960s, governments were already busier suppressing them, and the ruling classes — where ruling parties still existed and were not yet replaced by military warlords— were busy subordinating such parties to the state. While some political scientists were extolling the virtues of mass mobilisation in one-party democracies and political entrepreneurs were dogmatically emphasising the classless character of African societies, the military was taking over in one African country after another, calling the only shots of the day, and leaving political participation, this very important ingredient of democracy, as a false remembrance of things past in the pages of La Palambora and Myron Weiner (1966).

While the practitioners of public administration were asking whether the new ruling elites were developmental in their attitudes or whether they were much more swayed by primordial ties in making decisions, corruption was on the rise, governmental bureaucracies began to swell and burst at the seams, and very soon there followed bloody fights as to who was to occupy which bureau. Quite often, it was the colonel who shot himself to power who momentarily and at times almost perpetually (as in the case of Mobutu) settled the disputes. From then on, so as not to create situations for more disputes, politics remained banned. Talk of democracy or even of development in a place like Chad under Tombalbaye in the daily practices of government became purely academic. In many cases, any public discourse became a discourse of sheer physical survival.

Even where bureaucrats were reasonably well meaning and some economic growth could be ensured, by the mid-1970s political participation, public accountability, the rule of law and defence of human rights increasingly became rare commodities in the governance of African societies. In the Afro-Marxist states, such as Sekou Toure's Guinea, it was argued that the masses would enjoy democracy only after they had been liberated from poverty. In the meantime, the revolution had to be undertaken by the party, in the name of the masses, by denying any form of political power to the bourgeoisie and other privileged social classes (Wamba-dia-Wamba 1987). Mengistu Haile Mariam was later to follow in the same manner when he clothed a military dictatorship in the garb of a workers' party in the years following the overthrow of Haile Selassie (Giorgis 1989).

By the end of the 1970s, government in Africa was already assumed to be something to be discussed within the realm of technocracy: there was a concentration on the socio-economic consequences of the way in which state power was used in the continent. Anxious to demonstrate the Marxist thesis that in capitalist society, in the words of the Communist Manifesto, the state is nothing but a committee for managing the common affairs of the whole of the bourgeoisie, Marxist scholars of various shades and persuasions searched for national bourgeoisies, comprador bourgeoisies and the like, hoping to find the extent to which they used state power to further their interests as opposed to those of the popular masses. The political economy approach, concentrating on the context of politics more than the politics itself, and emphasising political outcomes rather than political contests, became predominant in the left's discussion of African politics.

Thus, for example, Colin Leys' *magnum opus* (1975) on Kenya's political economy after independence does not mention the word democracy in the index. Christopher Clapham's introduction to *Third World Politics*, emphasising the context of politics in his analysis, gives no place to democracy, as seen in the total absence of this concept in the index. Says Clapham (1985:1):

> What makes politics of the third world in some measure distinctive is not the nature of the peoples and politicians who take part in it, but the nature of the circumstances in which they find themselves: and what is unfamiliar may thus for the most part be readily understood by anyone prepared to try

to appreciate those circumstances and the kinds of action to which they are likely to lead.

Harry Goulbourne (1979) equally ignores the issue of democracy, and again the concept does not feature in the index. We could go on with further examples.

But it should not be ignored that the political economy approach played an important role in liberating social thinking and analysis of politics from being something in which individuals simply played roles, and that these roles were somehow related to system maintenance and continuity which, in the context of developing countries, was important in giving the government the leeway to undertake development or modernisation; to something in which individuals were social actors embedded in concrete experiences which gave them their being. The behavioural approach assumed the neutrality of the government or political system in political action, not to mention that it was oblivious to the context (domestic, international, structural, etc.) in which politics took place. It was political economy which brought in the socio-economic dimensions into the study of politics while unfortunately underplaying the subjective factors in political struggles.

The State Becomes a Burden

By the beginning of the 1980s, discourses on development began to emphasise that the state was becoming a burden to development in Africa. In other words, developmental dictatorships had failed in Africa. Elliot Berg's famous World Bank study (1981) posed this as a largely technocratic problem. Bureaucracies were too large, governments were too wasteful, planning was not properly done, urban dwellers were favoured in public expenditure, prices were not right, and farmers had no incentives. The responsibility of politics in all this was conspicuous by its absence in the discourse, and the emasculation of democracy in African political *praxis* was not even broached.

The OAU's *Lagos Plan of Action* (1980), appearing just before the World Bank study, did no better. If anything, it lingered more on the international context *à la dependencia* of Africa's woes of underdevelopment.

While these two documents were not really meant to be discourses on politics, they are important in that they discussed issues which were highly germane to African politics, and they heavily influenced this discourse in the 1980s. The issues continued to be discussed in largely technocratic terms until the Third World Forum started its series on 'Studies of African Political Economy', which led to the publication of our book, *Popular Struggles for Democracy in Africa* (1987). In the introduction to that book, I emphasised the need to understand the character of the distribution of political power in Africa and the shutting-out of the people from the arena of politics so that the state could pursue policies which had led to the underdevelopment of African economies. Only democratic revolutions would bring the people back to the centre stage of politics and determine a different character for the use of state power, this time more likely in the popular interest.

All the essays in that book looked at the different experiences of African peoples in struggling to come back to the centre stage of politics, and the strategies adopted by ruling classes and African states in politically oppressing and economically exploiting the people. Few examples of liberal democratic experiences are cited; they are notable by their absence. Where participation is tolerated, it is without its corollary of control and accountability, and it is done within the political terrain of the dominant social classes so that certain forms of oppression are legitimised or rationalised, as in Uganda, Swaziland or Kenya.

In other cases, where 'purist' ideologies have been used to legitimise oppression, quite often invoking Marxism-Leninism as the reigning ideology, the upholding of democratic rights has been sacrificed at the altar of persons asserting the scientific truth and moral superiority of their official doctrines: Marxism-Leninism in Congo under Nguesso, Benin under Kerekou, Guinea under Sekou Toure and Ethiopia under Mengistu; humanism in Zambia and the third universal theory in Libya (Sklar 1982).

Democracy and Popular Participation

Wherever we turn, no African experience after independence shows that democracy was actually sacrificed for a more positive outcome or for development, for that matter. Nor was it guided by enlightened despots who knew what they were doing. The debate that has raged since the late 1980s has therefore revolved around the following issues:

- What has been the African experience with democracy?
- Is there a uniquely African version of democracy?
- What case can be put for democracy in Africa today?
- Is democracy necessary for development?
- Can African societies, as they are today, sustain democracy?

The first question has been adequately dealt with in this essay. The second however, needs some critical attention. The argument that the one-party system derives its legitimacy from African traditional society, however eloquent Nyerere's and Sekou Toure's arguments were, has been adequately laid to rest: both Nyerere and Toure were involved in false analogies (Anyang' Nyong'o 1991). The experience of Africa also shows the consistently non-democratic character of one-party systems: it would be difficult to make a case to the contrary where history has already proved otherwise. Thus Nyerere should have given his commissioners a greater latitude for discussing if those democratic principles could, in real terms, be realised and sustained under a one-party system and not foreclose the discourse before the commissioners started their work.

There is, indeed, a case to be put for democracy in Africa today; it is a philosophical and moral case before it becomes a political and economic one. Philosophical and moral because questions of why people should subject themselves to some form of authority have always been ethical and moral. Social Contract theories, in the Holy Bible as well as among the French philosophers, down to Locke and Mill, emphasise the importance of the individual in society, and the whole purpose of social existence as being that of promoting the greatest good of the greatest number. This is done not by submerging the individual interest within some kind of mass interest defined by some social or political power external to the individual, but by making the individual an active participant, consentor and creator of the total whole.

The political and economic case to be put for democracy can be advanced at two levels: one is the fact that almost all constitutions on which independent African states were established were democratic. Although practice rarely matched aspirations, the people still cherish these aspirations and struggle for them. No other agenda seems worth pursing except that for which independence was fought. The struggle for democracy is still the centre of the agenda for the liberation of the people.

Notes
1. At that time the goal looked remote; within five years only the white settler colonies in Lusophone and southern Africa remained intact.
2. These issues later led to the split between the radical nationalists (who joined the Kenya Peoples' Union) and the conservatives (who remained in KANU) (Anyang' Nyong'o 1989).

References

Anyang' Nyong'o, P, 1987, *Popular Struggles For Democracy in Africa*, London, Zed Books.

------------, 1989, 'State and Society in Kenya: The Disintegration of the Nationalist Coalitions and the Rise of Presidential Authoritarism', *African Affairs*, 88, 351, April, 229-51.

------------, 1991, 'The One Party State and its Apologists: The Democratic Alternative', Nairobi Law Monthly, August.

Bitek, Okot p', 1989, *Song of Lawino, Nairobi*, Heinemann, Kenya Ltd.

Clapham, Christopher, 1985, *Third World Politics: An Introduction*, London, Croom Helm.

Cliffe, L, (ed), 1967, *One Party Democracy*, Nairobi, EAPH.

Decalo, Samuel, 1986, 'Military rule in Africa: Etiology and Morphology', in Baynham, S, (ed) *The Military in Africa*, London, Croom Helm.

------------, 1990, *Coups and Army Rule in Africa. Motivations and Constraints*, London and New Haven, Yale University Press, 366 p. [Second edition].

Emerson, Rupert, 1960, *From Empire to Nation*, Cambridge, Mass., Harvard University Press.

Giorgis, Dawit Wolde, 1989, *Red Tears: War, Famine and the Revolution in Ethiopia*, Trenton, The Red Sea Press.

Goulbourne, H, (ed.) 1979, *Politics and States in the Third World*, London, Macmillan Ltd.

Huntington, S, 1968, *Political Order in Changing Societies*, New Haven and London, Yale University Press.

La Palombra, J, and Myron Weiner, 1966, *Political Parties and Political Development*, Princeton, Princeton University Press.

Leys, Colin, 1975, *Underdevelopment in Kenya: The Political Economy of Neo-Colonialism,* Berkeley, University of California Press.

Macpherson, C, B, 1973, *Democratic Theories: Essays in Retrieval*, Oxford, Oxford University Press.

Mboya, Tom, 1963, *Freedom and After*, London, Andre Deutsch.

Mohiddin, Ahmad, (n. d.), *East African Journal*.

Nkrumah, Kwame, 1957, *Ghana: The Autobiography of Kwame Nkrumah*, London, Panaf.

------------, *Towards Colonial Freedom*.

Nyerere, J, 1963, *Democracy and the Party System*, Dar-es-Salaam, Government Printers.

------------, 1968, 'Socialism and Rural Development', in *Freedom and Socialism*, London, OUP.

Oginga Odinga, Jaramogi, 1967, *Not Yet Uhuru*, London, Heinemann.

Organisation of African Unity (OAU), 1980, *Lagos Plan of Action*, Addis Ababa, *Panaf* 1973 Great Lives, Patrice Lumumba, London, *Panaf*.

Shivji, Issa, 1970, 'Tanzania: The Silent Class Struggle', paper given at East African Social Science Research Conference, University Dar-es-Salaam.

Short, P, 1974, *Banda*, London, Routledge and Kegan Paul.

Sklar, Richard, 1982, 'Democracy in Africa', Presidential address, African Studies Association, Washington, DC., November.

Wamba-dia-Wamba, E, 1987, 'Popular Struggle for Democracy in Africa: The Case of the Peoples Republic of Congo', in Anyang' Nyong'o (ed.).

World Bank, 1981, Accelerated Development in Sub-Saharan Africa, Washington DC.

4. Democratic Theory and Democratic Struggles

Mahmood Mamdani

Are there similarities evident in democratic struggles in different African countries? Can some of these be summed up more accurately as shared weaknesses? If so, to what extent do these arise from a failure to conceive adequately democratic tasks and objectives under today's circumstances?

In this paper, we explore some of the weaknesses in democratic movements that arise from a tendency to treat democratic theory as received wisdom. We are concerned with two specific expressions of this tendency to deal with theory as if it were a frozen artifact, rather than as a body of thought in continuous formation.

In the first part, we trace a key shortcoming in contemporary democratic movements to a failure to question two central notions in the 'European' and 'American' tradition of rights: of the 'nation' as the bearer of the 'right to self-determination', and of the 'citizen' as the bearer of individual ('human') rights. To show that the specific context of contemporary Africa requires us to rethink these salient features in rights theory, we begin by demonstrating how these very features developed earlier in response to definite historical contexts.

A second set of weaknesses in contemporary democratic movements flows from the failure to come to grips with a more recent history: that of the wave of struggles that followed the close of the Second World War and the corresponding colonial reform that sought to contain and diffuse these. Key to this reform was a restrictive notion of democracy which defined rights as political (and not civil or social). The pluralism that was the result of the post-war colonial reform was narrowly political, but not social and ideological. While granting the freedom to organise political parties, this reform introduced a web of supervisory controls on social movements; by cutting the link between political and social movements, it tamed political parties into state parties. Present-day democratic struggles tend to conceive of democracy just as narrowly. By equating democracy with multi-parties and dictatorship with single-party regimes, these movements risk a reform as limited and as precarious as that of the post-war decades.

Rethinking Some Salient Features of Rights Theory

Rights Theory in the European Context

At its core, rights theory in Europe came to coalesce around two points of agreement: contemporaries generally came to agree that the nation was the bearer of the collective right of self-determination, and the citizen the bearer of individual rights. Though the two strands are intimately connected in their development, flip sides of a single coin, each has a distinct history.

The historical context of rights theory in Europe was the struggle of middle classes against the feudal-evangelical order. From the Renaissance to the Enlightenment, notions of divine right gave way to those of national sovereignty (Chailand n.d.:19-20);[1] the 'source of all sovereignty,' declared the Revolutionaries of 1789 France, 'is essentially the nation'. True, there raged a debate among liberals and conservatives as to who constituted 'the nation'. Liberal and rationalist thinkers saw the nation as a political category of freely associating individuals; they formulated one or another theory of 'social contract'. To this broadly democratic conception, conservative and romantic thinkers opposed one or another version of an organic theory of nationalism; nations, they argued, are not created but have basically an inherited and traditional character (Cohen 1944; Mamdani 1988).

Whatever their conception of the nation, contractual or organic, all sides agreed that the right to self-determination belonged to the nation. By the time 'wars of national unification' engulfed nineteenth-century Europe, the fusion of nationalist and statist notions — of nationalism and patriotism (Strayer 1970)[2] — crystallised as a consensus: that the rightful destiny of every nation was to establish its own state, and that the legitimate political authority in human affairs was the nation-state. Once the nation was accepted as the legitimate bearer of 'the right to self-determination', the debate on rights now appeared as a debate on nationhood. The debate on whether Jews or Armenians or Poles were a nation was really a debate about whether they had a legitimate claim to the right of self-determination, i.e., the right to establish their own nation-state.

The notion of collective rights that grew out of nineteenth-century European struggles was essentially statist: the other side of the notion that the nation was the legitimate bearer of the right to self-determination was the assumption that the fullest exercise of this right required that a nation establish its own state, the nation-state. It is worth noting that a wide range of political theorists in nineteenth-century Europe — be their persuasion liberal, conservative or socialist — shared this premise. So, for Marx and Engels, as for Hegel, peoples without states were peoples without history.[3] The 'self-determination of nations,' Lenin clarified, 'means the political separation of these nations from alien bodies, and the formation of an independent state'.[4] Socialists in Europe wrote tomes on whether Jews were a nation with the legitimate right to self-determination.

Stalin's book on *Marxism and the National Question* was considered the definitive treatise on the subject in the social democratic movement. Of the five criteria he put forth defining a nation, one was that of 'a common economic life', the result of generalised commodity production. In other words, Stalin argued and the socialist movement accepted that nations are the product of capitalist development; conversely, there exist no nations in pre-capitalist colonies. The constitution of the Soviet Union distinguished between three types of national groups in a hierarchical fashion, each with its corresponding set of rights. At the top of the hierarchy were 'union republics' inhabited by 'nations' which were considered 'sovereign'. Then followed 'autonomous republics' whose population did not meet all five of Stalin's criteria and were thus not considered sovereign. At the bottom were 'autonomous regions/areas' inhabited by 'nationalities'; their rights were the most limited (Chailand n. d.:102-3).

While the debate on 'nations', 'nationalities' and 'national minorities' within Europe was a lively controversy, its flip side was once again a point of consensus. All were agreed that there were no nations among colonised peoples. And this was assumed to be particularly true of Africa. For Africa was a land of 'tribes', not nations. Unlike nations, tribes were presumed to have no social history. Their existence in time was quantitative, not qualitative. A compilation of occurrences over that time could generate a chronology of dates and events, but not a history; whereas the movement of such a chronology was at best cyclical and repetitive, the stuff of historical movement was progress. The premise that all sides to the debate on national self-determination in Europe shared was that 'peoples without history' (Wolf 1982)[5] have no legitimate claim to rights!

The circle was complete. Those who lack a social history can only possess characteristics which are innate and primordial. While it may be futile to attempt a historical sociology of these peoples as one could of nations, it was possible to study tribes using the tools of an ahistorical anthropology. Stripped of its social basis, the history of struggles of colonised peoples to control their own destinies — in other words, the history of their democratic struggles — could easily be interpreted as some kind of a pathological response of 'tribes'. Thus the overloaded nature of the term 'tribalism' in the literature of anthropology and political science, as some kind of a coming to surface of the real nature of the 'native', stripped of the veneer of civilisation![6]

One would have thought that the development of a theory of human rights would have effectively countered the statist definition of the 'right to self-determination'. For, after all, throughout seventeenth-century England and eighteenth-century France, liberal thinkers tried to arrive at a system of fundamental individual rights which the state is not allowed to invade (Laski 1962:69). As formulated from the seventeenth century, the core of liberalism could only be defined as a theory of individual rights and limited government (Macpherson 1973:172). And yet it is ironic that in its attempt to define a ground for 'rights' that cannot be violated by the state, liberal thought became circumscribed within a state-defined logic! (Boli 1987) For liberalism, the bearer of individual rights came to be 'the citizen', a member of the political community defined by the state. The French Revolutionaries of 1789 entitled their manifesto *The Declaration of the Rights of Man and of the Citizen*. Contemporaries argued over whether citizen's rights should be confined to the male gender, or whether they should also be extended to women. Critics pointed out that the conception of citizenship was limited also in a second sense: the rights embedded in the Civil Code of 1790 were restricted not just to men but to 'men of property' (Laski 1962:147-9, 127).[8] Later, militants from within the anti-colonial movement would demand that the colonised be treated as 'citizens', not 'subjects'.[9] But, whether liberals or Jacobins (Jordan 1985), male supremacists or feminists, colonisers or colonised (Shivji 1989:46),[10] while they argued over how far the definition of citizenship may be restricted or stretched, all agreed that rights be the prerogative of the citizen!

This is why it is not difficult to read the history of human rights as a history of citizen's rights, especially as one goes up the familiar chronology of the three principal types of rights: civil, political and social/economic.[11] Fully developed by the end of the eighteenth century, civil rights,[12] especially when defined as 'inalienable', most clearly restrict the authority of the state and uphold the autonomy of the individual. But even these are limited as citizen rights, with the state usually holding 'emergency' powers to suspend them under such conditions as war, natural disaster or internal subversion. Crystallised in the nineteenth century, political rights[13] are clearly meaningful only for the citizen. And, finally, social and economic rights[14] — except for the right to private property,[15] ideologically inspired by the French Revolution but practically realised only after the Russian Revolution of 1917 — clearly resume the existence of strong state intervention in citizen affairs (Marshall 1948, 1964; Boli 1987).

The assumption that rights should be restricted to citizens holds for both the more conventional African Charter on Human and Peoples' Rights, adopted by the 1981 OAU Summit, and its radical predecessor, the Universal

Declaration of the Rights of Peoples of 1976, otherwise known as the Algiers Declaration. The African Charter states the principle clearly: 'Every citizen shall have the right to participate freely in the government of his country...' In one of its more far-reaching articles (Article 7), the Algiers Declaration proclaims that 'every people has the right to have democratic government', but then proceeds to qualify 'democratic government' as one that 'represents all the citizens without distinction as to race, sex, belief or colour, and capable of ensuring respect for the human rights and fundamental freedoms of all'! (Shivji 1989:100-12)

Rights Theory in the American Context

The dividing line in American constitutional thought and rights theory is the Civil War. Before the Civil War, the paradigm of rights that prevailed in the United States was that received from the European tradition. It is the Civil War that compelled American theorists to look their own reality in the face. The resulting innovations in American constitutional thought were a significant departure from the European tradition.

It is well known that the Civil War was about the 'right to self-determination', and not the abolition of slavery.[16] When is the claim by a group to establish an independent state an exercise of the right to self-determination, and when is it secession? In the American Civil War, the matter was settled by force; with its defeat, the Confederate cause came to be defined as 'secession'. But the defeat of the South was also the defeat of the principle of the 'right of nations to self-determination' in American constitutional thought.

It was Lincoln's genius to recognise that what was distinctive about the American experience was the dispersal of nations and not their coming together.[17] For America, unlike Europe, was a settler country. From the settler point of view, self-determination as a right of nations jarred on two counts: not only did it have little relevance to a settler population of multi-national origin, it also raised the uncomfortable question of the right of the indigenous population to self-determination. Hence, the significance of the shift, in US constitutional thought, from the 'right to self-determination' of nations to the 'right to non-discrimination' of individuals. This outcome not only preserved the integrity of the Union, it also undercut the legitimacy of any demand for self-determination by the indigenous inhabitants of the United States, the Indians.[18]

In addition, it signified a decisive shift in emphasis from collective to individual rights. For the right to self-determination is a collective right; that to non-discrimination is an individual right. As the American discourse on rights began to move away from any notion of collective rights to a single-minded elucidation of individual rights, it also began to disassociate the discourse on rights from that on power.

But the conceptualisation of individual rights in the US has also another, and a positive, side to it. In granting Federal citizenship to blacks and Indians, the Thirteenth Amendment shifted the locus of citizenship from individual states to the Federal Government. This introduced a new element in rights theory: in the States of the Union, the claim to rights was no longer based on citizenship, but on residence (labour).

Though contradictory, the result was full of possibilities: on the one hand, a move to a highly individualist notion of rights as US constitutional thought abrogated the right to self-determination for nations;[19] on the other, the uneasy coherence of two contradictory bases for rights— one in citizenship (Federal), the other in residence (State)— was a step towards repudiating the statist notion of rights in liberal thought.

Rights Theory in the African Context

At the end of the Second World War, the UN Charter proclaimed the right of 'self-determination of peoples' and 'human rights'. We have tried to show above that there is no single and unambiguous notion of who should be the bearers of these rights: who are the 'peoples' and the 'humans' whose rights are being proclaimed? Instead of thinking that all that is involved is taking hold of a pre-existing notion of rights so as to 'apply' and 'respect' them, one needs to begin with an understanding of what is unique about the African context to arrive at a notion of rights adequate to it.[20]

As a first step to underlining Africa's specific experience, it should be obvious that Africa is not Europe. In Africa more than in any part of the world, there is little coincidence between the history of nation formation and that of state formation, between social history and political history. Many state boundaries in Africa date, not even from the Berlin Conference of the 1880s, but from the decade of independence of the 1960s. More than the outcome of internal social histories, they reflect the exigencies of external geopolitics.

By and large, the states in Africa are not nation-states. What goes by as nationalism in most African countries is predominantly a statist ideology; some observers have even been led by this to comment that, in Africa, it is the state which has set out to create a nation! (Chailand n. d.:2) And yet, the presumption that 'the right of nations to self-determination' is of no relevance in Africa because nations do not exist in the continent can no longer hold. For, one may ask (Mamdani 1976:3), what is it that makes 8 million Swedes a 'nation' with the right to self-determination, and many times more Hausas a 'tribe' with no such right; or 4 million Norwegians a 'nation' and 8 million Baganda a 'tribe'? Or, for that matter, fewer than a million Icelanders a 'nation' and no fewer Langi a 'tribe'?

Is the point then to turn things upside down and argue that since every 'tribe' in Africa is a 'nation', every African nation should have the right to self-determination? Or is it rather to note that the terms 'nation' and 'tribe' are overloaded and emotive precisely because the former has been considered the legitimate bearer of the right to 'self-determination', but not the latter? How many have forgotten that, when the struggle for Eritrean independence was raging, its legitimacy in African intellectual circles hinged on settling one key question: is Eritrea a 'nation' or not? If the question was settled in the affirmative, the Eritrean demand for a separate state became a legitimate struggle for 'self-determination'; if not, it could be denounced as an illegitimate attempt at 'secession'!

Of one development, there can be little doubt. Faced with state repression, which was often unleashed in the name of national unification, democratic struggles inevitably give rise to demands for group rights. A case in point is developments in the Horn of Africa. The nineteenth-century European solution to such demands was to recognise the 'right of nations to self-determination', meaning the right of every nation to set up its own state. If Africa is to recognise as just the demand for group rights, can it afford to duplicate the European solution and interpret this as the right for each national group ('nationality', 'tribe') to set up its own state? Has the attempt to solve the question of 'national minorities' in Europe— that of Poles, Armenians and Jews in an earlier period, and Serbs and Croats today— by setting up a separate state in which the 'national minority' can be turned into a 'national majority', worked?[21] Or has it served simply to proliferate 'national minorities' in Europe?

My point is that the solution to the question of 'tribalism' in Africa can be neither to declare these demands as 'illegitimate' and settle them by force, nor to christen 'tribes' as 'nations' and call for the establishment of a separate state for each. The point is to query the very assumptions from which follow both solutions: that 'self-determination' must mean, in the final analysis, the setting-up of an independent state. As a second step to coming to grips with the concrete experience that is Africa, we need also to underline that Africa is not the Americas. There is no country within Africa with a settler majority. Even South Africa is not a USA, though the settler minority would have liked to impose an American solution whereby the right of an individual to non-discrimination obscures the difference between the colonial-settler minority and the colonised-indigenous majority and is observed at the expense of the right of collective self-determination of that majority.[22]

There are two distinctive features about the shape of social reality in Africa. One is that Africa, like the Arabian peninsula, is a land of migrant labour. The political economy of a number of countries in the southern half (Lesotho, Mozambique, Swaziland) was shaped by migrant labour. In West Africa, colonial powers moved large masses of populations from the semi-arid inland (the Sahel) to coastal plantations; even today, over two million Bourkinabe migrant labours live and work in Cote d'Ivoire. On the eastern side of the continent, the out-migration of impoverished peasants from Rwanda and Burundi has been a parallel development; as early as the 1950s, nearly 40 percent of the population of Buganda comprised Banyarwanda immigrants.

The outcome of migrant labour is a radical rupture between the land of one's birth and the site of one's labour; and, as a result, between the country of one's citizenship and that of one's residence. Since 'human rights' in liberal theory flow from membership of a political community ('citizenship') and not of a labouring community ('residence'), this single fact has been sufficient to strip millions of migrant labourers of their 'human rights' legally. Only when the injustice meted out has been extreme and dramatic has it come to public light, as illustrated by the expulsion of Ghanaians from Nigeria, or Rwandese from Uganda.[23]

It would be a mistake to think that this question has never surfaced in democratic struggles in Africa. During the guerrilla struggle in the Luwero Triangle — which is residence for a large number of Banyarwanda migrants in Uganda — the National Resistance Army (NRA) linked the exercise of rights in village-based resistance committees to residence, rather than to citizenship. In the recent multi-party election in Cote d'Ivoire, while the opposition remained unwilling to recognise rights of Bourkinabe migrant labour, it is the regime in power which had the pragmatism to champion the right of migrants to vote and thereby incorporate their struggle into its own project![24]

The statism of liberal theory has created a sharp disjunction between the rights of citizen labour and the lack of rights of non-citizen labour. Isn't it ironic that while South African efforts to strip citizen labour of rights (through apartheid) were universally considered illegitimate, its denial of the rights of non-citizen migrant labour (e.g., immigrants from Mozambique) seldom came up even for public discussion? Is it not this fact which shaped South African attempts to solve the question of apartheid by creating Bantustan citizenship, that is, by 'de-citizenising' all migrant labour in South Africa, and thus legitimately stripping it of rights?

Our point is simple. Where the social history of peoples and their political history largely coincided, as in nineteenth-century Europe, citizenship served to enfranchise labour. But where the two histories are divergent,[25] to base rights on membership in the state community is to create a situation whereby citizenship serves to disenfranchise people. The African context is one where the liberal notion, of rights as an attribute of citizenship, has increasingly anti-democratic consequences. To change this situation requires rescuing rights from the narrow shell of citizenship, and linking it to the more universal fact of labour (residence).

Liberal theory is formulated around two constructs: citizenship and the market, one an artifact of political life, the other of economic life. Whereas liberalism as a theory of the market has universalist claims, at least in theory, liberalism as a theory of rights does not. Its statist character is underlined by two related claims: one, that the right to self-determination is not possible in the final analysis without the establishment of a state; and two, that the bearer of 'human rights' be a member of the political (state) community. One argument of this paper is that both these claims need to be re-examined for meaningful democratic reform in the context of contemporary Africa.

Pluralism and Democracy

If there is one demand which sums up the perspective of contemporary oppositional movements in most African countries, it is that for multi-partyism. While it no doubt expresses a popular demand for a change of regime, to what extent can the call for multi-parties be equated with that for democratic reform?

Multi-party politics first came on the African scene in the period after the Second World War. It was introduced as part of the colonial reform that sought to stabilise and contain a situation made fluid by widespread popular struggles. Detached from wider reforms that would guarantee social and ideological pluralism in public life, the introduction of multi-party politics was simultaneously an opening and a closure. We believe the experience of the three decades that followed the post-war reform in Africa shows the closure to have been of a more lasting and injurious effect.

There is an uncanny resemblance between the post-war reform of the 1950s and the democratic transitions unfolding in many an African country today. Today, more so than ever, the presumption in public life is to equate multi-party politics with democratic reform and single-party politics with dictatorship. Since single-party regimes have been widely discredited, should this simple equation continue to prevail, it will simply serve to keep from public debate a discussion of the full range of reforms without which pluralism in public life will remain an elusive goal. To make the point, let us return to the period of the post-war reform.

The single party that came to power at independence had its roots in the nationalist movement that gelled in the post-war upsurge. Long before the nationalist political party took the helm, the ground was rocked from under colonial feet by popular protest. One only needs to recall the spate of general strikes, from Ghana (1937, 1938), to Sudan (1945), to Nigeria (1946), to Dakar (1945, 1946), to Tanganyika (1947), to Zanzibar (1947), to Mombassa (1948), to Uganda (1945 and 1949), to Guinea (1953). No matter how limited their numbers, the significance of worker action was widespread—because worker struggles were embedded in broadly based popular struggles. As a political movement, nationalism did not emerge out of a void; whether it was the CPP in Ghana or TANU in Tanganyika, its organisation took place on a terrain richly textured with a variety of social movements and a history of social protest. To understand the resilience of nationalist protest, one needs to recall that the political movement was anchored in and nourished by a broad range of social movements.

A variety of organisations acted as vehicles of social protest—from trade unions (usually the general union), peasant cooperatives and religious societies (open or secret) to self-help associations (for loans or burials, for women or youth) (Mamdani 1988: 47-70). It is these social movements that mobilised different social groups around concrete social issues, and thereby prepared the ground in which nationalist political movements (or parties) came to be popularly anchored.

The cutting edge of the colonial reform that followed was to drive a wedge between political and social movements. The point was simultaneously to contain social movements and to sever their link with political movements. Once adrift, political movements were easily reshaped by their middle-class membership into state parties whose objective was limited to organising for periodic electoral contests.

The same reform that legalised social movements—such as trade unions, cooperatives and friendly societies (which were usually defined to include religious and self-help associations) — required that they be officially registered. Rules of registration enabled the state to supervise movement finances and approve their rules of operation. The point of supervision was to depoliticise social movement activity and professionalise its leadership. Ultimately, it was to replace forms of popular accountability by those of bureaucratic accountability.

Supervision and control through legal registration was extended from social organisations to the popular media. Since the radio remained a state monopoly, this was of significance particularly for newspapers. The very reform that looked like a political opening, since it allowed multiple parties to contest for state elections, turned into a closure from a social and ideological point of view.

Our point is that the reform of the 1950s was a contradictory movement. Emancipatory in its immediate impact, its long-run significance turned out to be negative. Though pluralist in its claim, the reform presented pluralism only in its political aspect, and equated political pluralism with multi-partyism. It was a deft movement which served both to emancipate and to muffle: while introducing political pluralism, it undermined social and ideological pluralism. It drove a wedge between political and social movements, with opposite results for both; its realisation led to a flowering of political parties but a wilting of social movements. It is in this contradictory context that nationalist parties with a transformative agenda could be recast, usually from within, into no more than trade unions of professional politicians, their main objective restricted to organise to win regular electoral contests for state positions.

This trend was carried to its final conclusion in the single-party regimes that emerged in post-independence Africa. Whereas in the colonial period the autonomy of social movements was compromised through state supervision, under the single-party regimes it was liquidated as the single party established 'mass organisations' under its own tutelage. Whereas a state-controlled broadcast media coexisted with a state-supervised print media in the colonial period, both broadcast and print media came to be state-controlled under the single-party regime. Whereas the colonial reform presented pluralism narrowly as political, the single-party regime liquidated even that narrow expression of pluralism.

Can we afford to forget that the single-party regimes that ultimately outlawed any expression of autonomy in public life — whether in organisation (of cooperatives or trade unions or friendly societies) or in expression (through newspapers) — built on supervisory powers embedded in colonial legislation? Let us take the example of Tanzania. It was the Societies Ordinance of 1954 that gave the governor 'absolute discretion' to declare a society unlawful if in his opinion it 'is being used for any purpose prejudicial to, or incompatible with the maintenance of peace, order and good government'. It was these powers that the governor used in 1957 to declare the Korogwe, Pangani, Hendeni and Iringa branches of TANU 'unlawful societies' without giving any reasons. And it was these very powers that the chairman of TANU used to ban the Ruvuma Development Association, a remarkable instance of self-organisation by a peasant community in independent Tanzania (Shivji 1990:17).

That same language of 'public interest', 'good government' and 'peace' pervades the legislation introduced to undermine pluralism in the ideological sphere. Thus legislation in Tanzania empowers the registrar to refuse to register a publication in the interest of 'peace, order and good government';

the minister concerned to cancel the registration for the same reasons; and the president to prohibit a publication in 'the public interest!' (*ibid.* 13-16).

Seen from this point of view, the multi-party reform of the 1950s (just as the multi-party regimes that claimed to uphold it after independence) and the single-party regimes do not signify opposed alternatives: on the one hand pluralism, on the other, the lack of it. Rather, they appear as different points in a single continuum: the soil which nurtured the single-party regime was prepared by the multi-party reform. Both begin with a definition of pluralism that negates its social and ideological dimensions and limits it to its political aspect. The common heritage that one upholds and the other repudiates, but around which both revolve, is of pluralism so narrow that its safeguards are meaningful mainly to political professionals.

Today, this shared premise is boldly upheld in the simple equation that multi-partyism equals democracy, and single-partyism dictatorship! True, there have been opposition demands for pluralism that have not been narrowly political; for example, the demand by the opposition in Rwanda for an end to state monopoly over broadcasting media. But these have been few and scattered. As a rule, the tendency to interpret democratic pluralism narrowly to mean no more than party pluralism remains strong in oppositional movements between the Sahara and the Limpopo.

Varying Conceptions of Democracy

'To the extent that British colonial authorities permitted African representation and involvement in politics in the Gold Coast', observes Kumi Ansah-Koi (1987:61) in a survey of politics in Ghana, 'the two strata of African society (namely, the chiefs and the intelligentsia), which struggled for such a role for and on behalf of the mass of the colonised Africans did so under the banner of democracy'. When every contending interest presents itself under the banner of democracy, the criterion of democracy ceases to be particularly useful in distinguishing between different types of interests. It then becomes necessary, as a starting point, to distinguish between different conceptions of democracy.

Not too long ago, there was a consensus among Africanists that democracy was not on the agenda in Africa. This common conclusion was reached by a variety of routes. At one end was an argument widely shared in developmentalist circles: that economic growth and political participation are incompatible (Gendzier 1985).[26] At the other was the contention of dependencia theorists that democracy is simply not possible under conditions of dependency. Somewhere along the line were those who arrived at the same conclusion as an expression of sheer realism (Bienen and Herbst n.d.).[27]

There has been a dramatic turnaround in Africanist perspectives in recent times. The same circles who used to argue only yesterday that democracy was at best a developmental luxury, today uphold democracy as a developmental necessity! But the consensus in these circles is more apparent than real; though they employ a common vocabulary — democracy as accountability — there is no clear agreement among developmentalists as to what this single catchword signifies.

An influential interpretation of 'accountability' as a necessary ingredient for 'good governance' has been put forth by the World Bank. But the accountability the bank speaks of is limited to an anti-corruption drive; its terms of reference are for accountants and managers. Its concern is with efficient management, not with self-management;[28] neither the bank nor any of the architects of 'Structural Adjustment' ever think of suggesting that African leaders be accountable to their peoples not just for the funds they receive and spend but also for the policies they implement! (Mamdani 1991:13-14)

In contrast to the World Bank's perverted notion of democracy as efficient management is the restricted notion of democracy as multi-partyism. This notion has found favour among a wide circle of academic liberals. Even as consistent a theorist as Richard Sklar (1987), at one time advocating a richly textured vision of pluralism,[29] has moved to a notion which reduces pluralism to its political instant, and thereby to a notion of democracy confined to the accountability of rulers to citizens (Sklar 1983).[30]

It has been one argument of this paper that the restricted notion of pluralism as simply political, introduced by the colonial reform of the 1950s, has been key to the wilting of social movements and the taming of political parties into state parties in post-independence Africa. Popular political parties can neither be created nor sustained without the existence of a wide range of social movements in which they are anchored and to which they remain accountable; to create an environment favourable to a democratic culture is not possible without first ensuring ideological and social pluralism.

The second argument of this paper has focused, not on the contemporary debate on what should be the content of these rights[31] but on the question of who should be the legitimate bearers of these rights in contemporary Africa. Because the answer to this question will confer legitimacy on certain historical actors, and not on others, it will be vital in shaping the future of democratic struggles in Africa.

It is this question, that of the democratic subject, that has evaded most Africanist thought. This is why, in spite of a widespread conviction among liberal Africanists that democracy is a universal value of equal relevance to Africa, their quest to bring 'democracy' and 'the rule of law' to Africa reminds one of nineteenth-century liberals who presumed it to be their 'manifest destiny' to bring 'culture' to the Dark Continent. Ironically, this is a standpoint not very unlike that of Soviet communist parties which sought to bring socialism as a turnkey project to African converts! And yet, as to whether democracy, self-determination and independence in thought and life can be brought to someone as a philanthropic gift from outside is seldom an issue for discussion among them. Not surprisingly, the only issue on which a diverse gathering of North American Africanists could agree on was to call on their government to add a 'political conditionality' to the existing list of conditionalities, as a way of bringing democracy to Africa (Mamdani 1990:7-11).

But democracy is not an artifact that can be introduced and sustained regardless of context, either as an intellectual enterprise or as part of a foreign aid package. The guarantor of democracy cannot be constitutional safeguards engineered by consultants, but the organised presence of social and political movements which need democratic freedoms for their very existence, and which will therefore struggle to defend them.

Faced with the Africanist consensus outside the continent and the multi-party chorus inside, the response of most progressive African intellectuals has either been a pragmatic accommodation with the narrow demand that democracy equals accountability,[32] or an ambivalence to the demand for multi-parties.[33] While agreeing with pragmatists that our starting point has to be the existing movement and not some ideal substitute, this recognition of reality cannot be turned into a reconciliation with its limits. It is the theoretical premise of these limits— on the one hand the unarticulated assumption that the legitimate bearers of rights are the duality nation/citizens, on the other the narrow equation of democracy with multi-partyism— that we have tried to explore and question in this paper.

Notes
1. A crucial step in this transition was the Reformation which, by nationalising religion and repudiating the transnational empire of the Church, helped to set the stage for the rise of the nation-state.
2. Strayer (1970) argues convincingly that loyalty to the state was not the same as nationalism. As with Germany and the Habsburgs, when the state was 'multi-national', conflict could rage between the two.
3. Marx and Engels distinguished between 'great nations' vital for historical progress, as opposed to 'little nations' without the intelligentsia and the bourgeoisie to develop that nation's own political, economic and cultural life (Chailand n.d.:122).

4. '... it would be wrong,' Lenin insisted, 'to interpret the right to self-determination as meaning anything but the right to existence as a separate state' (Lenin n.d.:20, 397).
5. Title of Eric Wolf, *Europe and the Peoples without History,* California 1982. Wolf wrote a history of imperialist exploitation of the Third World, but still assumed that the history of the relations between 'the West' and the peoples it colonised was the sum total of the history of the colonised peoples! For a critique, see Asad 1987: 594-607.
6. Take, for example, two sets of historical events of great emotive significance: the French Revolution and the Mau Mau rebellion. An episodic description of both would bring to light similar events: destruction of property, widespread disorder, death, etc. Put in the context of a broader social history, this chronology would gain a larger meaning; bathed in a deeper hue, these events could even become milestones in the unfolding of world-historical developments. Stripped of their socio-historical context, similar events appear as devoid of reason, bizarre and mindless, an expression of the irrational, as in numerous studies of the Mau Mau. While in one case violence and disorder may appear as the 'midwife of history', in another they stand as testimony to the darker and primordial side of tribal society!
7. Boli writes: 'The ideology of the expanding state while freeing individuals from traditional authority constantly co-opts the ideology of individualism by defining individuals in terms of citizenship and by translating human rights into citizen rights. This process of constructing citizenship, along with the inventory of citizen rights and national institutions, define the individual as member of the nation. Citizen rights are 'incorporative', serving not so much to strengthen the possibility of individual choice as to expand state jurisdiction over the lives of citizens, bringing individuals into the arena of state action and control' (Boli 1987:133-4).
8. Macpherson (1973) points out that 'classical liberal theory was committed to the individual right to the unlimited acquisition of property, to the capitalist market economy, and hence to inequality, and it was feared that these might be endangered by giving votes to the poor' (Macpherson n. d.:172-3).
9. Note, for example, the response of Senghor to Article 53 of the European Convention of 1950 which excluded the non-Metropolitan countries from its provisions. Senghor cautioned his fellow deputies in the French Parliament lest they end up preparing a Declaration of the Rights of 'the European Man'—which is exactly what they proceeded to do! See M'Baye and Ndiaye 1982, quoted in Shivji 1989:46.
10. Shivji points out the restrictive character of the notion of 'citizenship' as historically evolved, excluding at first 'women', then 'slaves' and then 'natives'. But one limitation that Shivji ignores is that inherent in the very notion of 'citizen: that of its opposite, the 'non-citizen'! (*ibid.*:46).

11. A different classification of human rights, suggested by the French jurist Karl Vasak, distinguishes between three 'generations' of rights: the first generation is civil and political rights, closely associated with the liberal tradition; the second is economic, social and cultural rights linked to the socialist tradition; third is a set of 'developmental' rights connected with the rise of the anti-colonial movement in the post-war period.

    This last right, defined in Article 28 of the Universal Declaration of Human Rights as 'everyone is entitled to a social and international order in which the rights set forth in this Declaration can be fully realised', can be described more as an aspiration than as a 'right'.

    The 'right to development' was first formulated by the Senegalese jurist Keba M'Baye and formally recognised by the UN Commission on Human Rights in 1977, followed by a General Assembly Declaration on the Right to Development in 1986.

    Noting that under this right the human person is seen as a 'participant and beneficiary' (Article 2 (1)) in a process of development that may be anyone else's project, Shivji has argued that 'the right to development fits in neatly in the ideology of developmentalism which has been the hallmark of African states since independence in rationalising the depoliticisation and demobilisation of the masses' (Shivji 1989:29, 83).

12. The so-called 'negative' rights of assembly, speech, movement, due process and freedom from cruel and unusual punishment.

13. The oldest of the so-called 'positive' rights: to vote, to hold office, to initiate legislation.

14. Those protecting the individual against 'poverty, disease and ignorance'.

15. In the words of Shivji: 'It is commonly said that while Western countries espouse the priority of civil/political rights, the Eastern bloc subscribes to the priority of social/economic rights. This division of rights has so much become a part of the Cold War and imperialist propaganda that debaters have often overlooked the fact that private property, so dear to the heart of the West, is an economic right' (Shivji 1989:52).

16. During the first two years of that bloody strife, the war aims of Lincoln did not include the abolition of slavery. Rather, Lincoln was prepared to guarantee the seceding states a constitutional right to slavery if that had to be the price of keeping the Union intact (Dahl 1991: 493).

17. I am indebted to discussions with Robert Meister of the University of California at Santa Cruz for this observation.

18. Majorities in the US are considered to be issue-based and temporary, not historical and permanent. Thus group theorists like Robert Dahl define modern democracy as 'a process of governance by which minorities — plural — rule' (Margolis 1983:119):

19. The obvious objection to this point is Woodrow Wilson's championing 'the right of nations to self-determination' on the morrow of the First World War. But this was clearly an exigency of foreign policy and had little to do with the rights discourse within the US. On the foreign policy front, upholding the banner of the 'right of nations to self-determination' allowed the US simultaneously to undercut the legitimacy of empires held by colonial powers and to stand alongside the newly established Soviet Union whose leadership argued that the right to self-determination in the twentieth century needed to be extended from nations to colonised peoples.
20. Shivji claims that key to 'revolutionising the human rights framework' is recognising the centrality of the 'right to self-determination' and the 'right to organise' (1989: chap. 3), and proceeds to sum up the 'principal element' of the 'right to self-determination' as the 'right of oppressed nations to self-determination up to and including the right to secession' (*ibid.*:80).

    The point that this formulation continues to beg is, first, who are the 'oppressed nations' in the African context? And, second, will the application of this nineteenth-century European principle (self-determination as every nation establishing its own state), no matter how consistently, solve African problems or multiply them?
21. In most African countries, in fact, there is no 'national majority'; does it make any sense to speak of 'minorities' in the absence of a majority? Does one then need a new political vocabulary to discuss the African experience meaningfully?
22. Whereby, in addition, a politically oppressed majority is divided up into several cultural minorities ('tribes') placated with inalienable cultural rights.
23. Note, for example, the lack of public outcry when millions of 'non-citizen' Yemenis — most of them residents of Saudi Arabi for four decades — were expelled from Saudi Arabia during the Gulf War; and the assumed legitimacy of the Kuwaiti situation where a 'non-citizen' majority labours without rights and a minority monopolises rights as 'citizens'.
24. Note, for instance, the controversy surrounding the rights of 'guest workers' in Europe. In a recent European Community treaty draft, the right of return of peoples of German descent, and the provision that this right be respected in every EC member state, contrasts sharply with the qualified rights of German-born children of Turkish labour migrants.
25. One needs to acknowledge that this divergence is not simply a fact of historical significance. The more contemporary fact that processes of political economy bear little relationship to state boundaries has reinforced rather than diminished this historical divergence.
26. Irene Gendzier has traced how, starting from a post-war point of convergence around 'democracy', North American social scientists soon took cover under the banner of 'order' as they were confronted with the real world of democracy through a variety of movements that challenged American hegemony in the newly independent countries of the world (Gendzier 1985).

27. For example, Bienen and Herbst concluded in a recent article that the 'most pressing problem in Africa is not how to create democracies but how to soften authoritarian regimes' (Bienen and Herbst n.d.:28).
28. Mkandawire ridicules this as a 'special brand of tropicalised democracy' reduced to the accountability by the state, leaving out such key aspects of democracy as freedom of association, freedom of expression, judicial protection and due process and respect of human rights' (Mkandawire 1991:4).
29. At one time Sklar insisted on a thick meaning of pluralism at various levels: multi-partyism, separation of powers to ensure pluralism within government, and economic and social pluralism (Sklar 1987:696-8).
30. On the basis of a narrow notion of accountability, of rulers to citizens, Sklar proceeds to distinguish between different types of democracies (ranging from 'liberal democracies', like multi-party Senegal, to 'guided democracies', like single-party Kenya, to 'participatory democracies', like single-party Zambia, to 'social democracies', like Nyerere's Tanzania), claiming that the only difference between these is the difference in 'the means of securing accountability'! (Sklar 1983:11-16)
31. Whether this debate is framed in terms of the content of pluralism (political, social, ideological) or that of rights, as signified by its three generations (civil and political, social and economic, developmental) (see note 11 above).
32. Thus, note Peter Anyang's inclination to think of democracy in terms of 'accountability' (see the exchange between Anyang' and Mkandawire in *CODESRIA Bulletin* 1 and 2, 1991).
33. Note, for instance, the ambivalence of Shivji to the demand for multi-parties in Tanzania. Neither opposing nor supporting this demand outright, Shivji only goes so far as to ask rhetorically whether it makes a difference to have power monopolised by two or three parties as opposed to one party (Shivji 1990:20). For an unequivocal stand on the question of multi-partyism and the right to form political parties in a democracy, see Ibrahim 1986:38-48.

References

Ansah-Koi, K, 1987, 'A historical outline of democracy in Ghana', in K, A, Ninsin and F, K, Drah (eds.), *The Search for Democracy in Ghana*, Accra, Asempa Publishers.

Asad, T, 1987, 'Are there histories of peoples without Europe?', *Comparative Studies in Society and History*, 29:3, 594-607.

Bienen, H, and Herbst, J, n.d., 'Authoritarianism and democracy in America', Princeton, mimeo.

Boli, J, 1987, 'Human Rights or State Expansion? Cross-National Definitions of Constitutional Rights, 1870-1970', in G, M, Thomas *et al.*, *Institutional Structure: Constituting State, Society and the Individual*, Berkeley, Sage.

Chailand, G, (ed.), n. d., *Minority Peoples in the Age of Nation States*

Cohen, H, 1944, The Idea of Nationalism, New York, Macmillan.

Dahl, R, A, 1991, 'Democracy, majority rule, and Gorbachev's referendum', *Dissent*, Fall issue.

Genzier, I, 1985, *Managing Political Change: Social Scientists and the Third World*, Boulder, Westview, Colorado.

Ibrahim, J, 1986, 'The Political Debate and the Struggle for Democracy in Nigeria', *Review of African Political Economy*, 37 December, 32-48.

Jordan, D, P, 1985, *The Revolutionary Career of Maximilien Robespierre*, Chicago, Free Press.

Laski, H, 1962, *The Rise of European Liberalism*, London, AMS Press.

Lenin, V, I, n. d., 'The Rights of Nations to Self-Determination', in *Collected Works*, 20.

M'Baye, K, and Ndiaye, B, 1982, 'OAU', in P, Alston (ed.), *The International Dimension of Human Rights*, Westport, Greenwood, Conn. et UNESCO, Paris.

Macpherson, C, B, 1973, *Democratic Theory: Essays in Retrieval*, Oxford University Press.

Mamdani, M, 1976, *Politics and Class Formation in Uganda*, New York, Monthly Review Press, Heinemann.

------------, 1990a, 'Reconceptualising the Birth of State Nationalism and the Defeat of Popular Movements', *Africa in the 1980s*, Dakar, Proceedings of the Sixth General Assembly of CODESRIA.

------------, (1990b, 'A Glimpse at African Studies, Made in USA', A Review of the Proceedings of the Inaugural Seminar on Governance in Africa Program of the Carter Centre of Emory University, February 17-18, 1989, *Africa Bulletin* 2:7-11.

------------, 1991, 'McNamara Speech: A Rejoinder', *CODESRIA Bulletin*, 2:13-14.

Margolis, M, 1983, 'Democracy: American style', in G, Duncan (ed.), *Democratic Theory and Practice*, Cambridge, Cambridge University Press, 296p.

Marshall, T, H, 1948, *Citizenship and Social Class*, Cleis, New York.

------------, 1964, *Class, Citizenship and Social Development*, New York, Greenwood, MACL.

Mkandawire, T, 1991, 'Democratic Governance in Africa', Dakar, mimeo, Dakar, June.

Shivji, I, 1989, *The Concept of Human Rights in Africa, Dakar*, CODESRIA.

------------, 1990, 'Pre-Conditions for a Popular Debate on Democracy in Tanzania,' paper presented to seminar on *Party System and Democracy in Tanzania*, Dar-es-Salaam, Tanganyika, Law Society, 27-28 September.

Sklar, R, 1983, 'Democracy in Africa', presidential address to the 29th annual meeting of the African Studies Association, Washington, DC., November 15, 1982, *African Studies Review*, 26, 3-4, September/December, 11-16.

------------, 1987, 'Developmental Democracy', *Comparative Studies in Society and History*, 29, 4:696-698.

Strayer, J, R, 1970, *On the Medieval Origins of the Modern State*, Princeton.

Wolf, E, 1982, *Europe and the Peoples Without History*, California, University of California.

5. The Economic Crisis, Adjustment and Democracy in Africa

Kankwenda M'Baya*

The Economic Model in Crisis

Symptoms of the Economic Crisis in Africa

The 1980s was a lost decade for Africa. In fact, it was during this decade that the economic crisis of the continent came to light. This crisis, however, was inherent in the economic structures in place and was therefore foreseeable.

The crisis was of 'unprecedented and unacceptable dimensions', as manifest not only in 'a terrible drop in economic indicators and trends, but also dramatically and flagrantly in the suffering, enormous difficulties and impoverishment of the vast majority of African people' (ECA n.d.).

At the economic level,[1] the annual average gross domestic product (GDP) growth rate for African countries was 1.3 percent between 1980 and 1989; the annual average production growth rate per sector fluctuated between -1.2 percent for the industrial sector and 1.3 percent for the agricultural sector. The attendant drop in annual average revenue per capita was more than -2 percent, representing a decrease of 30 percent over the same period.

Whereas in the 1960s the annual average GDP growth rate was about 2 percent, levelling out and stagnating in the 1970s for sub-Saharan Africa, this led to a continual reduction in per capita consumption in that the annual inflation rate (15.2 percent) was double that of the two previous decades.

In the same vein, investment rates in the region stood at slightly above 15 percent of GDP as against 20 percent in the 1970s. The low investment growth rate stems from the increased scarcity of resources through poor export results, stagnation or even reduction in the flow of external resources, greater and increasingly heavier debt-servicing obligations, and a series of austerity measures under Structural Adjustment Programmes (SAP) (Adedeji 1991a:24-5).

The average annual rate of return on investment dropped from 30 percent in the 1960s and 13 percent in the 1970s to 2.5 percent in the 1980s.

External relations are in no better shape. Africa remains marginalised in international trade as its export volumes continue to decrease, recording a significant drop from 4.7 percent in 1980 to 2.1 percent in 1989.

The regression in the prices of raw materials caused these indices to drop from 100 in 1980 to 63.5 in 1989. Whereas the continent recorded trade surpluses of US$1.8 billion and $19.1 billion by the end of the 1960s and 1970s respectively, the 1980s registered a major trade deficit of $7.1 billion.

Similar external debt trends have worsened to the point where they have become a serious obstacle to recovery on the continent. Debt remittance soared spectacularly from US$138.6 billion in 1982 to $260 billion in 1989, representing 93.3 percent of the continent's GDP. Debt servicing has thus increased considerably, reaching more than 32 percent of Africa's export revenues.

During the decade under review, six countries that had been defined as middle-income countries in the previous decade were reclassified as low-income countries. The number of Least Developed Countries (LDCs) rose from 31 in 1980 to 42 in 1989, with Africa accounting for 28 of them, representing two-thirds of the poorest countries of the world (UNCTAD 1989).

As regards food, the average calorific value dropped by 0.2 percent per year during the decade, and; 'contrary to the food situation elsewhere, the proportion of sub-foods increased during the eighties and their absolute number rose by 27 percent'. About one out of every three Africans is underfed. The failure of the development policies in place was 'established' as suggested by 'all institutions that examined Africa' (Saouma 1991). All these had a negative impact on access to basic social programmes for Africa's peoples, education and health in particular.

Many considered these economic factors briefly outlined above as the underlying causes of the economic crisis both at the level of macro-economic balances and within economic sectors.

However, limiting the analysis of the crisis to the scope of the macro-economic factors or the economic sectors, even if properly done, will not capture the full essence of this crisis, particularly with regard to its repercussions on other sectors. Such an approach would not also allow for efficient and sustainable solutions. It is for this reason that, in spite of the intervention of Africa's 'social partners' at the bilateral and mainly at the multilateral level (IMF, EDF, IBRD), the crisis has persisted, increasingly worsening, perplexing both Africa's decision-makers and analysts. It is against this background that we suggest the crisis is not exclusively economic, and that it must be approached from other angles.

True, the economic crisis is real and its impact can be felt at all levels of economic activity. Yet what is the African economic crisis? If it cannot be crystallised in one element or several factors put together, such as the deficit in public finances, imbalances in the balance of payments, the collapse of productive sectors or indebtedness, what then are African economies really suffering from?

Nature and Origin of the Economic Crisis

Our submission is that Africa's current economic crisis is one of an economic model — the accumulation model — and is therefore a crisis of the model itself or of the political components that established, managed and fed on the system (Kankwenda 1987). That is why the crisis concerns the entire economy which is affected both at the macro-economic and sectoral levels. It is also for this reason that the model is being challenged in the political arena, which is considered as a strategic ploy of the accumulation model, and also because it is possible to use the political arena as a forum for the expression of a collective struggle.

Suffice it to say here that the accumulation model is based on the system of articulation between the economic sectors of a country. These include determining the sectoral basis of accumulation, being the economic surplus generators to fund global or sectoral economic development, setting-up of transferable surplus levels as well as transfer mechanisms and the use of such surplus. These reflect both the alliances and struggles between classes and sub-classes of society.

It is for this reason that when a model runs out of steam, or falls into a crisis, the entire economy as well as the dominating class alliances which flourished on the system are also plunged into crisis.

In a nutshell, the accumulation model comprises the following characteristics:

- The agricultural and industrial mining sectors are the two sectors upon which the model is built. Agricultural surplus is transformed into financial capital, essentially through the fixed price mechanism. Since prices are set at a level lower than value, the share of unpaid value is directly converted to industrial capital for agricultural production for industry, and indirectly to the entire financial capital for the remaining marketable agricultural production through low salary schemes, depending on the possibility to pay from food-crop produce.
- This allows for substantial capital profit margins and the attendant major possibilities of self-financing investments. Agricultural surplus is also transferred to the state through cash taxes and other in-kind and in-cash obligations. The mining surplus is transferred to the state

through taxation and dividend-sharing (the state is usually a shareholder in most of these enterprises), but it is mostly absorbed by capital for purposes of internal and external accumulation;

- Most of the economic surplus is used as financial capital abroad through unequal exchange mechanisms and not internally: the deterioration of terms of trade and transfer of revenue. The locally consumed surplus is mainly used by the state to finance economic and social infrastructures, and to self-finance industrial enterprises;
- The agricultural sector is the base of internal accumulation. We are not referring here to a conscious and deliberate accumulation, but to forced accumulation. The accumulation is said to be mandatory because of the constraints of state mechanisms: taxation, unequal exchange conditions and the deterioration in terms of trade in the agricultural sector. In other words, there is no surplus swapping between the agricultural and the other sectors, but rather there is a levy on the agricultural surplus, without any returns deriving therefrom accruing to the agricultural sector itself.

In case of mandatory accumulation, farmers are exploited and forced to cut down on their consumption to provide for and meet the requirements of industry and other sectors deriving benefit from the agricultural surplus, through taxation and the deterioration of trade terms in agriculture. This is tantamount to depriving the farmer of self-financing facilities likely to sustain his development.

This situation has a negative bearing in that it hinders the development of other sectors which appropriate or use agricultural surplus. 'Industrial development' through mandatory accumulation in agriculture may be quite rapid at the beginning. Industry is not required to give of its own resources in the exchange with agriculture since grain is produced automatically: steel is put back into steel. But as industry develops, its base, which is agriculture, tends to diminish.

The collection of the agricultural surplus is an impediment to the expansion of Africa's production, or at least limits the scope of such expansion; accordingly, it makes it more and more difficult for the farmer to produce enough surplus to meet the needs of industrial development. Where there are no other accumulation sources, a crisis sets in. 'Mandatory accumulation has destroyed accumulation at the source' (Poulain 1977:155).

We are referring here essentially to subsistence farming. Export-oriented agro-industry generally falls under 'capital', and the surplus generated by this sub-sector is to a large extent absorbed by capital. It is for this reason that export-oriented agro-industry generally commands the full attention of the dominant coalition: agronomic research, low salary policies, tariffication policy, transport networks, loan facilities, etc., to which peasant farmers do not always have access.

The model as painted in broad strokes above does vary from one country to another. It depends on whether the major economic activity is agriculture or mining, thereby determining the nature of dominant capital; and on whether the dominant coalition (the state and financial capital which is essentially foreign) is controlled by a bureaucratic or militaro-bureaucratic class, a coalition of classes lacking specific economic bases (the case with most African countries), a political class with commercial overtones (the case of Nigeria), or a class with agro-peasant connotations (the cases of Cote d'Ivoire, Kenya and Cameroon).

This colonial model has not really been challenged since independence. Only the officials charged with running the model have changed at the national level — the officials who made certain arrangements and political alliances depending upon the nature of the national economy and the decolonisation process in various countries.

Over the thirty years during which Africa has 'autonomously' managed the system, two other new phenomena can be noted. Public or private commercial capital (supervisory companies) developed significantly and became a partner in the dominant coalition, controlling the food and even non-food surpluses by marketing part of the export products, particularly agricultural, as well as industrial supplies.

Finally, without being fully in control of the rules of the game, and less so of national production capital, the state authority does not control the accumulation process. It neither defends the sectors generating economic surpluses (with a few exceptions in North Africa), nor did it lay down the modalities for transferring surpluses to finance other sectors.

The continental application of this accumulation model has effects on the two major sectors of agriculture and industry. In fact, from the colonial days to date, agriculture has continued to be plundered to finance and run other sectors without surplus swapping or retention of a substantial share of surpluses for agricultural development itself.

The two consequences which have resulted are that, on one hand, agriculture has stagnated or regressed, while on the other industrial growth has almost come to a standstill. The market is in fact limited, agriculture and the rural world having been bound to reduce consumption. Furthermore, self-financing opportunities for industry have been reduced, as agricultural surpluses at its base have reduced rather than increased. The system was thus plunged into crisis, with both agriculture and industry unable to develop.

The increase of commercial capital finally absorbed the accumulation ratio linking subsistence agriculture to industry and urban capital in general.

Production costs for industrial capital therefore continued to increase (salaries, supplies and spare parts, for example) whereas the industrial market shrank further. The haphazard development of commercial capital thus became an obstacle to the development or accumulation of industrial or financial capital.

In order to eliminate commercial capital from these activities or at least reduce its disastrous effects on accumulation in certain African countries, capital then moved into agricultural activity for the local market, stepping in as a direct producer by servicing worker canteens or urban markets, or providing assistance to farmers with a view to industrial supply. In several countries, this tendency towards the elimination of commercial capital was accompanied by measures to liberalise the agricultural sector.

In the mining industry, on the one hand, production costs increased given the weak agricultural surplus and its appropriation by commercial capital, thereby reducing any surplus it might generate. On the other hand, a good part of the surplus was appropriated and used abroad by major foreign capital via several channels already referred to, while most of the mining surplus remaining in the country was shared between the state and the mining industry itself.

The mining sector, which had become the principal base for accumulation in certain countries, therefore ended up hardly receiving anything for self-financing its operations. Hence it was plunged into ongoing crisis, attenuated from time to time by increases in the prices of raw materials.

The entire system therefore is in crisis, given that there are no other sources of accumulation. Accordingly, the major production sectors experience the crisis either as stagnation or regression while the main macro-economic balances, namely demand and supply, balance of payments, public finances, prices and revenue, are offset.

The current economic crisis in Africa is therefore a crisis of the accumulation model in that the model is at a dead end: it is collapsing, and is unable to regenerate. There is as yet no clearly defined replacement model in place to be implemented.

A critical analysis of the situation, be it in mining or agricultural countries, reveals that this model is characterised by the overriding role of exporting raw material as the main function, without any solid base for internal accumulation likely to offset or attenuate its collapse should a crisis set in. In other words, accumulation which made it possible to finance development in Africa over the past thirty years was sustained by the export of raw materials from the soil and sub-soil. This applies generally to Africa—despite the apparently contrary examples of the profitable exporting of jeans from Morocco or shirts from Mauritius.

In as much as African countries do not control the networks for the external realisation of their economic surplus, even this accumulation base will remain shaky and above all limited. The continual deterioration in the terms of trade has only further reduced the possibilities of accumulation. Accumulation has thus been said to have failed, or reference is made to the bankruptcy of the comparative advantage theory based on the exportation of raw materials. Having brought their countries to this crisis level, African leaders were no longer able to stop the crisis from impacting the political and social sectors of society.

The Political Component of the Model

The limited nature of the base of accumulation of this model is not only economic but also social. It is a model of exclusion and not of participation.

Therefore, at the socio-political level, the survival of the accumulation model leads to the limitation of the social base of development and preoccupations about the social and human dimension of development. In other words, but for a few exceptions, the model has ushered in political structures that are unitary, totalitarian, paralysing or unproductive, with a view to containing the other forces within a certain measure of control. It is thus only another form of what has been referred to as 'the colonial production mode'. This to some extent obliges the political structures in place to give primacy to certain economic structures deriving from exports. This surplus arises from the functioning of the model and not from development.

By crushing civil society, African states made it impossible for such society to be itself, i.e., something different from the caricature of the totalitarian and autocratic state. Similarly, by systematically stifling the upsurges of creativity likely to have spontaneously sprung from the various components of society, African states ultimately limited their chances of social and economic development, thereby condemning themselves to stagnation. For there is no creative state without a creative society, and *vice versa*. The collapse of the economic system in Africa is therefore:

> largely the result of political and social conditions on the continent, characterised by poor administration, lack of public accountability, and the non-participation of the majority of the people, further reduction of the decision making base, the confidence crisis between the government and the governed... The transformation of the entire political economy into an economy of despotism where authoritarianism and cleptocracy replace democracy, responsibility of public authority and political empowerment, have not only negatively impacted on individual freedoms, but have also even marginalized individuals in the development process, the result being that, in the heat of it all, the population has been entirely forgotten (Adedeji 1991b).

The political component of the economic model did not provide any political role for or significance to the people as a whole. In most countries, the abrogation of economic and political power from the primarily sovereign people translated into the emergence of the single party which rapidly became a toy in the hands of dictatorial presidents who modified or corrupted the constitution to maintain themselves in power.

As McCarthy has noted:

> Furthermore, once the fundamental equilibrium of power guaranteed by the constitution was threatened, the other checks did not take long to collapse: human rights are neglected, freedom of speech is abandoned, and political opponents are imprisoned. The legislative assemblies became rubber stamp institutions, the judiciary lost its independence and no longer rendered justice, in fact, at least as far as the business of state is concerned (McCarthy 1991:80).

In spite of and contrary to the ideological inclinations of African political regimes, the entire continent was run by 'strong regimes', with few exceptions, since they were all political components of the same economic development model, of the same mode of insertion in the global economy and thereby of political systems which essentially were the watchdogs of the metropolis.

That is why this model was neither sustainable nor self-sustaining in Africa; and that is why the 'miracle' and 'take-offs' clamoured for did not happen at all. The reduction of the external accumulation base, particularly following the deterioration of terms of trade and the drop in export production and productivity in this sector, no longer allow the model to function. It is therefore plunged into a crisis for want of other sources of accumulation. Hence the crisis of this model is not only a crisis of economic structures, but also one of political structures.

The debt crisis — the inability or incapacity to respect payment deadlines — which resulted was both component and warning signal of the generalised crisis, and it shifted attention from macro-financial balances and management problems. Debts entered into for purposes of financing development were transformed into debts for underdevelopment.

Who then is guilty? Those who accepted this model for Africa and who were its torchbearers and who were in positions of leadership and managed it while refusing the endogenisation of accumulation and the broadening of the social base of development are guilty. Those who proposed it, promoted it and imposed it on Africa; those who financed it, supported it politically and derived economic, political, scientific and other benefits from it are also guilty.

That is why the inefficiency of public investment so widely condemned in Africa is not an accident. The sellers and buyers of technology as well as those who guaranteed these investments are responsible.

Under these conditions, an attempt to resolve the crisis from the top by changing management instruments and policy, as has been the case with Structural Adjustment Programmes, cannot bear the expected fruit.

Structural Adjustment and the Exacerbation of Contradictions

Social Contradictions

Although the African economic and social crisis was accentuated in the 1980s, it began well before then. In fact, since independence, from one decade to the next, economic performance continually deteriorated in most countries. This is so because the real origins of the crisis were linked to the economic structures in place (the accumulation model).

Solutions to the crisis were put forth yet unequally implemented both at the level of the African countries themselves (the Monrovia Strategy, the PAL, priority programmes and other regional and sub-regional programmes) as well as internationally (UNPAAERD, for example). But the Structural Adjustment Programme and its various components was the solution which had the greatest impact because of its effective implementation by the majority of countries and because it enjoyed the theoretical, financial and technical support of donors.

In fact, whenever local African programmes were prepared as a solution to the crisis which generally affected the structural conditions of the accumulation model, the donors, namely the International Monetary Fund and the World Bank in particular, proposed counter-solutions and refused to lend support to the African programmes. Their grounds were that, given the poverty of African states, the African solutions would never see the light of day.

SAP as a donor solution was therefore easy to impose. But, as opposed to the proposals put forward by Africa, the SAP only grasped the manifestations of the crisis in terms of internal and external imbalances—namely, deterioration of terms of trade, higher budget and balance of payment deficits, galloping inflation and the depletion of hard currency reserves.

The reform measures and economic policy instruments propounded by the stabilisation and adjustment programmes essentially focused on the manipulation of exchange rates through devaluation, control of the money supply and credit to the state or to the economy, interest rate policy with a view to encouraging external savings and judicious allocation of resources, tax policies aimed at reducing public expenditure and financing credit, liberalisation of trade and payment regimes as well as freeing-up of prices of goods and services.

The results were mediocre if not disastrous (ECA n. d.): growth rates continued to drop, financial balances remained fragile, the net flow of capital was detrimental to Africa, the local private sector remained menial, poverty and unemployment increased, the food deficit went up, the inflation rate rose as true price pertained, the rate of school enrolment dropped, infant mortality increased, while the major epidemics (trypanosomiasis, malaria, etc.) resurfaced, as the state was subjected to budgetary discipline in terms of debt servicing.

The credo therefore was one of 'all markets' but the measures taken on the contrary reduced popular demand and led to the shrinking of the national market for mass consumption goods and services. This did not revitalise the production apparatus but rather killed it.

The President of the Development Commission of the European Parliament put it so well when he said:

> The development or structural adjustment criteria of the Bretton Woods institutions are perfect for Sweden but are completely outlandish for a country like Zambia or Mozambique. I said it publicly at the joint assembly in Kampala. Let us stop the massacre. For there is no country where it has been successful, at least as far as the people are concerned. Why? Statistics indicate that over the past ten years there has been a permanent transfer of capital from the poorest countries of the world to the richest countries (Saby 1991:60).

The onus of adjustment as much as that of the crisis has been borne mainly by the population through significant reduction in internal public spending with its attendant grave economic and social consequences. African peoples expected their governments to build bridges and roads, schools and dispensaries; to stabilise their currencies, support the private sector, improve housing, create jobs, stimulate agriculture and stock breeding, etc. These are all expectations that governments were not able to meet under SAP.

Without solving the problems of the crisis, even if only at the economic level, Structural Adjustment Programmes put forth by donors as a solution to the African crisis has had the effect, on the one hand, of further impoverishing the populations of these countries, and on the other of facilitating capital flow towards donor countries.

In so doing, SAP exacerbated the social contradictions which existed prior to the introduction of the accumulation model currently in place and prior to the crisis which now makes it impossible for the leaders to hand out emoluments and other annuities to their political clients. While SAP might be a bitter pill to all people, the political class continues to lead the same lifestyle. This further isolates it and creates social tensions in society. At last, however, some African leaders have understood this phenomenon.

In fact since 1988, Mobutu of Zaire, who for more than two years received congratulatory messages from the IMF because his government constantly respected the performance criteria of this institution, formally revolted against the institution and declared he had another contract that was even more important to him—the contract with his people. He realised his people could not live on the glory of compliments from the IMF and the World Bank alone.

Also, Bongo of Gabon, from whom the Bretton Woods institutions required a second salary cut operation, also revolted against it in the early 1990s, arguing that those people were out to get his head.

Criticism of the Model and Democratisation Requirements

Structural adjustment is the last straw that broke the camel's back. Its presence made it possible to unleash the latent dissatisfaction and to channel and express this dissatisfaction in a less dispersed manner. The painful decade of economic decline is thus at the base of the protest movement. In fact,

> for several years, the standard of living of most Africans dropped more than ever before; salaries dropped in real terms, farmers received truly insufficient prices for their produce, schools and dispensaries were abandoned, and the number of unemployed youths continued to increase in the cities. In all these countries, several people pointed a finger at state management, accusing the state of corruption and revolted by its indifference.
>
> The sudden increases in prices led to social unrest in Nigeria, Morocco and Zambia. The inability of the government of Benin to pay civil servant salaries for several months sparked off strikes and political protests. In Nigeria, a reduction in university scholarships also sparked off the first student protests. In Cote d'Ivoire, workers reacted sharply to government's intention to levy a solidarity tax on all workers of the public and private sectors. The significant reduction in oil revenues recorded in Gabon translated into austerity measures, 'barricades', confrontation with the police and strike action.
>
> A good portion of the population established the link between economic difficulties and absence of fundamental liberties. For not having taken part in the political decision making, they did not feel obliged to accept or entertain any further sacrifices which obviously were unequally shouldered. Urgent but localised grievances were in a very short time transformed into popular criticism of the system established by government (Harsch 1991).[2]

This list above is indeed not exhaustive. To the population at large, structural adjustment was an austerity policy imposed by the leaders in power with the complicity of their donors who were presented as national saviours. Opposition to SAP therefore was not just a matter of challenging the policy, but also protesting against all those who defined, funded and implemented it, whether national leaders or their foreign partners. The process completely left out the population to whom policy-makers turned only to ask for sacrifices.

As we have argued elsewhere, Africa's tragedy today is that the people seem to be 'excluded' from the growth process in that they were left out from the booty during the good times but were being called upon, almost exclusively, to make sacrifices as things got tough. And yet they were expected to shut up, accept the burden and wait for the better tomorrow promised them, in which nobody believes any more.

The weight of the crisis could have been much lighter for everybody if benefits had been made and distributed equitably. For the quest for economic and mainly political stability, using the adjustment of the existing model under crisis as a pretext, has led to a situation where political institutions have become personalised, totalitarian and unproductive. It is all these factors that are being challenged (Kankwenda 1990).

Three levels of challenge must be identified: the first is the challenging of the accumulation model which is in crisis; the second pertains to the very definition and implementation of adjustment as a solution to the crisis; and the third relates to the elaboration and implementation of economic policy decisions such as SAP.

Yet adjustment has addressed none of these issues but rather focused on the not-so-liberal management 'techniques' of the leadership. With dissatisfaction becoming such that it may swirl into a hurricane and sweep away the model and its political component, it became obvious and urgent to confine such opposition to the decision-making process as much as possible. The very success of adjustment depended on African people accepting its effects.

That is why the democratisation requirement was rapidly interpreted as a need for the people concerned to participate in the making of political and economic policy decisions, so as to contain it within these limits. The acceptance of political pluralism was therefore like opening up a pressure cooker to let out some of the steam and pressure and thereby contain a possible explosion. That is why the proponents of adjustment have even raised it to a conditionality in the granting of aid, with a view to imposing it upon their allies, i.e., the African leaders who have not yet understood it all.

The controversy caused by the model and its political component are therefore reduced to the challenge implied by the democratisation requirement through political, trade union and media pluralism.

This all bears a strange resemblance to the independence struggles of the 1960s which were the challenge of one order to set up another, whereby political leadership reverted to the nationals.

All this happened as if Africa were entirely responsible for her mishaps. After having mapped and pointed out the way to development (the model now in crisis), sold and financed the most inappropriate programmes, lent support to the political systems required by this type of development, the international financial system, faced with the scope of the crisis and the attendant dangers, realised that Africa is a dead weight and saddles her with total responsibility for her misfortune and lays down some measure of democratisation as a conditionality for intervention. What then, indeed, is democratisation in Africa?

Democratisation of African Society

Economic Significance and Policy Requirements

It is obvious that one must not stop seeking solutions to the crisis, but rather go further to lay the groundwork for a new endogenised model for economic and social development — a model based on a function of conscious and internal accumulation grounded on a broadened base for social development.

The internalisation and consolidation of the accumulation base must be the prime focus for sustainable long-term development in Africa. This is the only sure guarantee for Africa in the absence of the colonial or economic domination of other regions of the world. The nature of the model implies that the sectors at the base of the accumulation are not seeking to export values but rather to exchange surpluses with other sectors with a view to providing sustainable development.

The broadening of the social base for development requires not only the establishment of 'conscious exchange relations', i.e., the surplus swapping among the various components of the population of their economic production, but also their full participation in the development process, both in its economic and socio-political dimensions.

That is what the African people are calling for. The transformation they are clamouring for involves not only the internalisation of economic development but also of the corresponding socio-political structures. The flag-bearers of the new model can no longer entertain the same complicity which has accounted for the crisis of the current model. Such is the price for the quality of life of its peoples. It is accordingly that the basic economic needs (food, clothing, etc.) and social needs (education, housing, employment) can be made available to the majority of Africa's peoples.

At the same time, the expanding of the base for social development must be ensured. This means that sustainable growth is everybody's business. The old and the young, men and women, country and city, grass-roots communities and administrative or political headquarters, the state and private individuals alike must all be fully involved. All these categories must thus be motivated and mobilised accordingly.

This also implies the liberalisation of thought and speech, the elimination of mechanisms that paralyse individuals and communities, as well as political and economic decentralisation. One of the major lessons to draw from the evolution of Africa's socio-economic situation, as corroborated by events in Eastern Europe and even on other continents, is that the democratisation of society is a requirement of development.

Democratisation develops a spirit of emulation and competitivity; it liberates the creative potential of a people; it puts in place checks and balances against any abusive centralisation of thought, power and wealth; it ensures social self-control and stimulates economic and social progress while enabling the society to take charge of its own destiny.

Democratisation implies opening-up to debate, transparency in the management of public property, freedom of opinion and speech, and a separation of powers. All totalitarian societies, whether liberal or socialist, tend to be sterile and for that reason hinder economic and social progress, even if from time to time they are able to rally the population and accomplish some measure of economic growth. Over time, the indoctrinated people demobilise and the crisis sets in.

The new African state must restructure its political relations with civil society to restore creative potential to society. This calls for dialogue with civil society, acceptance of the democratisation of thought and power (political and cultural pluralism), as well as a decentralisation of the decision-making process to allow the participation of the various social strata involved.

The key components of all democracies—debate on and about the society, freedom of the press, transparency, separation of powers or power-sharing, freedom of political association and of course the possibility of alternating leadership — should not scare off anybody. They are the guarantee for stability and the foundation for lasting unity.

Thus is not just a fashionable ideal, it is both a fundamental requirement and a component of the content for Africa's long-term development. Such is the nature of the socialisation of development. The pretext of the existence of centrifugal forces through ethnic and cultural diversity to justify the maintenance of decadent political structures no longer holds water, given that ethnic and cultural pluralism obtains the world over. Furthermore, African people have reached the level of maturity that they can comfortably sit at the table of democracy.

The new African state can only but be an economic agent in a manner and at a speed of development specific to each country and to each sub-region. It must usher in a creative and democratic civil society.

As we all know, democracy involves the transformation of economic, political and social structures. Therefore, the democratisation of society cannot be successful where the political structures alone are transformed. In fact, the democratisation of political structures and institutions alone cannot be meaningful and cannot be borne by the current economic structures. It will be tantamount to a shoddy and unfinished job.

The democratisation of African societies therefore means that the African people must master their economic as well as their political and social structures. The question that must be raised here is to determine how the African people can control this process so as to make its content meaningful. How can Africa ensure that future economic development models are elaborated and executed on the basis of the needs and priorities expressed by the people while taking into account the socio-economic realities of the continent? (Drabek 1991)

For this to happen, democratisation must be effectively translated into participation in economic, political and socio-cultural power. At the level of action oriented programme planning, and particularly at the level of implementation, the participation of the population and their various grass-roots communities, organisations and associations is crucial for the economic and social development enterprise to be successful.

Beyond the need for them to be informed and sensitised, the population must be involved in its capacity as the object and beneficiaries of development. Base-level development activities and collective self-reliance at the local level are components of the socialisation of development.

Village or neighbourhood groups for public local interest activities, associations and cooperatives of farmers, craftsmen or other categories of small business, NGOs and credit unions, and women's associations are various forms of intervention by civil society, and as such their initiatives must be encouraged and even supported by the state.

The new development model not only requires that such collective participation structures should exist, but that they, as partners with the state and business, should have a say in the development of Africa. This is all the more important as participatory human investment, the valorisation and utilisation of human skills and resources must have at least the same importance as capital in the new development paradigm.

Constraints and Limitations to Democratisation

Adjustment was seen as the elimination of the defects of non-liberal or pro-liberal management to align it to the liberal ideal as desired and controlled by the rich countries through the Bretton Woods institutions, working as their collective manager for the countries to be 'adjusted'.

Elsewhere, the implantation of another development model, from the elaboration of its implementation strategies to its achievement, requires a social organisation of an unquestionable political dimension in as much as it involves the identification of needs, negotiation of priorities and decision-making through the successive phases of execution. This is understandable both at the level of the interests of the national collectivity and of the different economic and social forces comprising that collectivity (UNDP 1991).

As stated above, even where things appear to be the same, democracy differs, depending on whether it is a matter of adjustment democratisation or development of socialisation. The limits of each of these processes are clearly visible.

While the first model is based on integrated world trade, maximal growth of global revenue, international investment and financial profitability, the second on the contrary affords priority to the interests of the national collectivity, implying the submission of external relations to national priorities, collective and permanent social dialogue between the main interests of the major components of the national collectivity and, above all, the responsibility of the state, at all levels, both towards itself and towards the people it represents (*ibid.*).

The first limitation is obvious, particularly with regard to the process of democratising adjustment itself, and is inherent in all bourgeois democracy, which is actually situated in the political arena whereas economic life is not and cannot be democratised. This is valid both at the level of internal and international relations.

At the international level — and this is the second limitation — the rights of the people to self-determination and independence are easily granted, as well as the rights of countries to political equality; but such is not the case with economic rights. In fact:

> the economic rights of the people include the production and exchange of the products throughout the world on a just basis, and this is a right that entails fundamental contradictions. The GATT is also — and this is paradoxical — a blockage to liberal economic systems in that it is based on the law of demand and supply, with the market acting as the regulator. And as soon as there are dominant positions, the market and the regulator are blocked.

> We therefore find ourselves in a system which appears to be liberal but which in reality is one of the most severe economic dictatorship. As soon as the Bretton Woods institutions lay out the 'Chicago boys' programme in a debt-laden country, the country is only further stifled. 'The World Bank

and the IMF have been instruments of permanent strangulation for most countries at the economic level and consequently at the democratic level, and have also hindered the respect of human rights' (Saby 1991:57-8).

For Africa the logic remains the same because the implantation of capitalist exploitation and domination from the time of the slave trade to date has always amounted to a systematic refutation of democratisation.

In reality, the adjustment democratisation currently under way in Africa is, at the international level, essentially an adaptation or standardisation of political systems tending to globalise the economy. Democracy apparently is only acceptable to the powers-that-be within these limits.

At the internal level — and this is the third limitation — democratising adjustment itself is a political answer, and thereby partial, to a crisis which is total in nature, i.e., economic, political and social. Whereas the main forces controlling the economies of Africa remain external to Africa, the democratic arena simply appears as a movement in partial answer to the aspirations of the people so as to reduce tensions and continue the capitalist exploitation while completing the integration of the global economy. It is obviously for this reason that political transition, as if by chance, is generally confined to senior staff of international financial institutions: see the cases of Congo, Cote d'Ivoire, Benin.

That is why, contained within these limits, this democracy is supported and imposed as a conditionality by donors. That is why it is being developed as a liberal formula that can be transferred to Africa and whereby 'the new monocracies parade before the West seeking legitimacy, like beggars claiming to be democrats and looking for philanthropists or sellers of democratic formulae' (Bazunini 1991).

In this context, the current democratisation process in Africa may only end up creating a new generation of well-meaning despots charged with ensuring the 'well-being' of collectivities. They will continue to hold or confiscate real power to the detriment of the African people, while tolerating some 'Jack of Knaves' to make noise about political trade union and media pluralism.

The democratisation under way will only be successful for the African people if it has a political component of another development model. In its turn this other development model will only be beneficial to Africa's peoples if it is democratic and if there is socialisation of development. This means that the process must be negotiated by the different strata of African societies and conducted by the people, political and economically organised through dialogue and ongoing discussion on decision-making and implementation.

Notes
* The views expressed in this paper are those of the author and do not necessarily reflect the position of the UNDP.
1. The figures in this section, except where otherwise indicated, were obtained from the World Bank (1989) and Adedeji (1991a).
2. In Niger, for example, protests arose from trade union challenges to the structural adjustment measures, particularly the adjustment of the education sector by students.

References
Adedeji, A, 1991a, 'A lost decade for Africa', *Annuaire Jeune Afrique*.

------------, 1991b, 'Forum on Security, Stability, Development and Cooperation on Africa', Kampala, 19 May.

African Charter, n. d., 'The African Charter for Popular Participation in Development'.

Bazunini, W, 1991, 'Multipartyism, democratisation or neo-Mobutism', *Solidaire*, Brussels, 23 May.

Drabek, A, 1991, 'Democratisation: For Whom and by Whom?', Initiatives, Summer issue.

ECA, n. d., 'African Reference Framework for Structural Adjustment Programs for Socio-Economic Recovery and Transformation', Nations Unies, E/ECA CM. 15/6/Rev. 3, 64 p.

Harsch, E, 1991, 'Democracy in Africa', *Development Forum* 154, Kankwenda, M, 1987, 'The Economic Crisis in Zaire: A Crisis of the Accumulation Model', in M'Baya (ed.), *Zaire: What Destiny*, Dakar, CODESRIA, 261-281.

------------, 1990, 'Solutions for Long-term Development in Africa', Niamey, roneo.

McCarthy, S, 1991, 'African Development and Political Heritage', *The Courier* 80, July-August.

Poulain, A, 1977, *The Mode of Socialist Industrialisation in China*, Paris, Maspero, p.155.

Saby, H, 1991, 'Human Dignity as a Universal Value', *The Courier* 80, July-August.

Saouma, E, 1991, 'Agro-food: Known Remedies, Failed Promises', *Annuaire Jeune Afrique.*, 91, Annual Report on African States.

UNCTAD, 1989, 'The Least Developed Countries'.

UNDP, 1991, 'For a Renewal of Development Planning in Africa: A Synthesis'.

World Bank, 1989, *Africa South of the Sahara: From Crisis to Sustainable Development*, Washington, DC., World Bank.

6. Adjustment, Political Conditionality and Democratisation in Africa*

Thandika Mkandawire

African states are, in an unprecedented manner, buffeted by a wave of pressures from both domestic and external forces calling for wide-ranging and profound economic and political reforms. The economic reforms envisaged are usually in the form of Structural Adjustment Programmes (SAPs) almost invariably drawn up by international financial institutions, while the political reforms proposed usually take the form of multiparty democracy. The economic reforms have been taking place for close to a decade now, while the movement for political reform is of quite recent origin. However, whatever their sequence and differences in start-up time, the two types of reforms are now linked in the minds of both the general public and specialists. Or, at least, each now serves as the backdrop to the other, so that no coherent discussion of the prospects of one is possible without consideration of the other.

The link between economic and political reform is sometimes made in a causal manner in that reforms introduced in one sphere have provoked calls for reform in the other, or by the suggestion that certain economic reforms can only take place if specific political reforms are made and vice versa. In other cases the link between the two types of reform is seen as merely contingent: the SAP happens to take place at about the same time as the democratisation process, which was set off by events not related to the economy — the 'demonstration effect' of 'Glasnost' in Eastern Europe, the 'political conditionality' imposed by donors as a result of domestic pressures from human rights movements in their respective countries, the rise within African countries of social movements with new economic and political demands, and so forth.

Yet no matter what the source of the linkage is, the simultaneous occurrence of SAP and democratisation processes calls for careful and systematic exploration. There is a need to examine the compatibility and contradictions of the various economic reforms with the political programmes of the emergent political actors in the African political economic scene. More specifically, one should seek to answer such questions as: What are the implications of the simultaneous pursuance of

SAPs and reforms toward multi-party democratic rule? How compatible are these objectives? What weights do different groups attach to these economic and political reforms? What are the domestic and foreign interests behind these changes and what content do these interests give to these reforms? What is the balance of forces between the groups pushing the different political and economic agendas and what, given the constellation of social forces in a specific country, will be the final 'mix' and its stability?

This chapter will attempt to address some of these questions, if only in an exploratory manner since the process is still unfolding and subject to rapid and unprecedented shifts in both content and direction.

The Domestic Origins of Political Reforms

The domestic sources of calls for political change are twofold: on the one hand, the changed political scene and the emergence of a whole range of social movements which are making demands on the political system in a manner that is unprecedented since the heyday of the struggle for independence; on the other hand, the impact of the economic crisis on the political perceptions of the state by these forces. Only a year or so ago one would have been hard put to identify social movements whose responses to the crisis were addressed not only to a set of specific policies, but also to the nature of the state itself and the processes of policy formation in Africa. Indeed, the rather passive way in which obviously painful austerity measures were received in much of Africa had begun to persuade some analysts that the political dangers of unpopular measures to the state had been 'overblown' (Bienen and Waterbury 1989). Presumably, the long-suffering African societies could be forced to swallow more of the bitter pill without fear of widespread protest. And if there was any protest it would assume the 'exit' rather than 'the voice' option, to use Hirschman's terminology (Hirschman 1970), or would be so diluted by all kinds of parochial schisms and patron-clientalistic commitments and loyalties as to be rendered politically impotent. Indeed, prior to the resurgence of social movements calling for democracy, there was a fascination on the part of certain groups for 'withdrawal' from the terrain in which the state was preponderant towards other areas far from the reach of the state—association life, parallel markets, ethnic associations, and so on. Considerable attention was focused on 'survival strategies' of households or social groups outside the reach of the state and the consequences of such withdrawal on the state structures. For some, the existence of such space for escape regrettably weakened the state (Hyden 1980), while for others such a possibility of escape was evidence of the vibrancy of African civil society (Chazan and Rothchild 1987). In both cases, however, such escape suggested the absence of social forces within civil society that would pursue democratic struggles in the arena that really mattered — the political arena.

During the last few years there has been an upsurge of movements which not only protest against the effects of adjustment policies, but are also calling for greater democratisation of their societies, greater accountability in the management of national affairs, and an end to corruption and waste, leading some to talk of an 'African Spring'. The social base of these movements remains unclear. However, one common feature is that thus far they have been basically urban-based and largely drawn from the 'formal' sectors. Contrary to some predictions, these social movements are quite 'traditional'. Trade unions, university staff associations, student movements, professional associations and urban church groups have in one way or another and in various degrees been involved in these upheavals.

In addition, demonstrators and rioters have included the ubiquitous and amorphous urban 'unemployed'. In a surprising number of cases, these movements have demonstrated remarkable resilience in the face of violent military repression. The Malian and Togolese movements are outstanding examples in this respect. Four days of rioting in Mali in 1990 in the face of an army that opened fire, killing 160 people and wounding 1000, led to a coup d'état and the overthrow of Moussa Traore. Since then the country has held democratic elections.

The political clout of these movements is reflected in the fact that they have dramatically changed the political landscape of a number of African countries. In most countries, the governments have retreated or indicated a willingness to re-examine the political structures of their countries, especially the one-party rule that has characterised most states. In some important cases these urban groups have constituted themselves into powerful electoral coalitions that have emerged victorious after general elections. This has been the case in Zambia, Benin and Cape Verde, where the one-party regimes have been abandoned, free elections held and the incumbents have accepted defeat. In Côte d'Ivoire and Gabon, multipartism has been rather grudgingly accepted and the opposition sits in the national assemblies, albeit uneasily. Kenya, Niger, Angola, Nigeria and Mozambique have all promised to hold free elections. In a number of countries, however, the process has been stalled due to the resistance and machinations of the incumbents: this is the case in Cameroon, Zaire, Togo and Burkina Faso where, as one member of the opposition has pointed out, an 'assassinocracy' still rules. In a typically British way, the former British colonies of Uganda, Ghana, Sierra Leone and Tanzania are going about the whole business in the roundabout and superfluous way of Commissions of Inquiry whose terms of reference are tantamount to sounding out the public on whether or not they seek to be free. There are, of course, some deafening silences in countries such as Sudan, but the general direction is toward some kind of democratisation of African societies.

The problems of the economy and the policies adopted to deal with the crises have contributed to the resurgence and cohesion of these otherwise disparate movements. They have also exposed the weakness and undermined the legitimacy of the state. There is no presupposition here that there is monotonistic relationship between economic policies and political manifestation. Rather, the point is that the economic conjuncture has fuelled the various struggles for a wide range of goals, including some which are not necessarily directly linked to the economy — human rights, ethnic identity, and so on.

First, macro-economic crises have brought to light long-hidden micro-inefficiencies and have highlighted the blight of corruption, especially as it has continued to provide enormous wealth to some while the majority is called upon to 'patriotically' shoulder the burden of austerity. Under periods of rapid economic growth, various forms of microeconomic inefficiencies in economic management can be lived with and overlooked. Indeed, they may even receive theoretical justification as essential engines of capitalism's macroeconomic dynamism à la Schumpeter. However, in times of crisis these same sources of dynamism become unendurable 'distortions', which are blamed for all that has gone wrong and cast light on a whole range of inadequacies hitherto neglected or condoned.

Secondly, the adjustment programmes have led to losses of post-independence gains in welfare which were part of the populist-nationalist programmes. The working class has witnessed a drastic reduction in real wages, which has been exacerbated by the removal of subsidies on wage goods, the introduction of 'user charges' on a number of public services and widespread retrenchment in the parastatal sector. In the most politically provocative cases, the state has simply not paid salaries over unbearably long periods of time. This has happened most frequently in countries belonging to the Franc-zone where the state does not enjoy the right to issue its own currency and cannot therefore resort to the printing press to pay salaries. The political and bureaucratic importance of regular payment of salaries, even in monies whose value has been scandalously eroded, should not be under-estimated. Failure to do so not only undermines the credibility of the state but interferes with the sense of routine that is so important to bureaucratic perception.

Thirdly, SAPs have contributed to the erosion of the populist programmes forged by nationalist movements after independence. The various coalitions that have provided a modicum of peace in much of post-colonial Africa were based on a complex web of redistributive policies, including food subsidies, pan-territorial pricing, regional planning and subsidised social welfare services. The political significance of these measures has been denigrated through being lumped together with or seen as tantamount to corruption ('rent-seeking', clientalism, patronage, and so on). But this is the stuff that political legitimation everywhere includes.

Finally, the package has dramatically compromised the position of the state as the bastion of national sovereignty and has revealed the State's weak and dependent character *vis-à-vis* foreign powers and institutions. It has raised the question as to whom the state is accountable. The assumption by foreign experts of key functions that have long been 'indigenised' is the most dramatic manifestation of this process. The African middle classes have had to suffer the indignity and humiliation of witnessing the reversal of indigenisation programmes as expatriates have reassumed certain key positions in government, the indigenisation of which had symbolised greater sovereignty by African states. This reversal has raised in a most dramatic way the issue of sovereignty and the real danger of multilateral recolonisation of Africa.

External Pressures: Political Conditionality and Adjustment

The most direct expression of foreign pressure on African states has been in the realm of economic policy. For more than a decade now African countries have been implementing SAPs, almost invariably designed and imposed by the international financial agencies. While those advocating these reforms claim that they are tailored to the particular needs of each country, they have generally involved devaluation of national currencies, drastic reduction in state expenditure, privatisation of state-owned enterprises and liberalisation of the trade regime.

While in the early years of the imposition of SAPs it was taken for granted that these programmes would be unpopular and would therefore require regimes that were insulated from popular pressures or had the 'political will' (to use the current euphemism for political callousness and insensitivity) to ride roughshod over such interests (Lal 1983), there has been a sudden shift towards a position that links structural adjustment to democratisation. So in addition to the 'economic' conditionality that plagued Africa during much of the 1980s, we now have 'political conditionality'.

It is important to emphasise that the external view on the necessity or appropriateness of democratic rule is very recent. It has been conventional wisdom that some form of authoritarian rule is a necessary, albeit painful, step towards development. It was part of the hard-headed 'No Easy Path' to development syndrome that reconciled many policy makers to authoritarian rule.

The turnaround in the West has been conditioned by a broad range of experiences, not all of which directly emanate from Africa. The first relates to the sweeping changes in Eastern Europe where economic and political liberalisation have appeared simultaneously on the agenda, in sharp contrast to the case of China where only economic liberalisation has been officially encouraged. It has therefore seemed only natural that Africa's own brand of 'perestroika' (structural adjustment policies) should be linked to 'glasnost'. Second, the parlous state of authoritarian governance in Africa has made a mockery of any form of economic assistance, as waste and corruption have eroded the basis for a rational economic use of resources. This state of affairs has been blamed on the lack of 'accountability' on the part of the authoritarian or patron-clientalist state. Hence the calls for some form of accountability that does not necessarily have to be democratic. It is also this that has forced international financial institutions and aid donors to address the question of 'governance', albeit in what is largely a technocratic manner. In its 1989 annual report, the World Bank (hereafter referred to as the 'Bank') clearly identified governance (defined as 'the exercise of political power to manage a nations affairs') as a central preoccupation. Although implicit in its pronouncement is a notion of democratisation, central to its preoccupations is the technocratic aspect of governance stressing 'capacity building' and economic growth. This has led Bratton and Rothchild (1991) to conclude:

> To date, the World Bank's fledgling governance programme concentrates on reducing the size of government, privatising parastatal agencies, and improving the administration of aid funds.

Third, the growth of human rights movements in the donor countries has contributed to this recent turnaround in the West. These movements have striven to inject human rights issues into both bilateral and multilateral aid programmes and have therefore called for some kind of political conditionality. In a number of countries, governments have been forced by these domestic movements to begin to link continued economic assistance to better performance in the political realm, including a shift towards multipartism, respect for human rights, and so forth.

Fourth, and undoubtedly most importantly, have been the political upheavals in Africa itself. A number of donors have been shaken by the realisation that the regimes they have thus far backed are on shaky grounds. To curry favour with the new movements, some donors have had to make sharp turns in policies. In some cases, the turnabout has been mainly aimed at recapturing the political initiative.

Finally, changes in intellectual perceptions have been important in the development of views on the appropriateness of democratic rule. More specifically, there is an accumulating number of (statistical) analyses suggesting that there is no evidence of an unambiguous relationship between political regime type (democratic or authoritarian) and economic growth (Sorensen 1991). This evidence has been used to question the related argument that authoritarian regimes are more capable of initialling the kind of economic reforms entailed by SAPs. It has also led the World Bank (1991) to conclude:

> On the whole the evidence suggests that the democratisation-authoritarian distinction itself fails to explain adequately whether or not countries initiate reform, implement it effectively or survive its political fall-out.

It is, from an intellectual history point of view, interesting to note that this 'evidence' is invoked and has apparently become most persuasive during the current political climate when it indeed seems most urgently needed. This coincidence should in itself cast grave doubts upon the association of democracy to specific economic aggregates for it suggests great political malleability of statistical analyses. It also points to the danger of allowing economic metaphor to dominate political discourse as well as the potentially ephemeral nature of commitment to democratic governance when it is tethered to a particular economic model.

Potential Sources of Conflict

At first sight, it would seem that the calls for democratisation by the internal forces dovetail neatly with the demands by the donor community for greater accountability and democratisation. Recent World Bank reports have been hailed as signalling a major shift in the donors' perspectives away from a preference for technocratic-authoritarian regimes toward an endorsement of the need for greater accountability of African states to their own people and greater democratisation of decision-making processes. Yet, as we will argue, things are not that unambiguous.

One should not take the commitment of all donors to democratisation at face value. There are at least three factors that will tend to blunt their commitment: the inertia of habit; the nature and the imperatives of economic interests of major donors in particular countries, and; the political economy informing the donors' perception of policy-making in Africa.

Inertia and the Loss of Sovereignty

On the inertia side, there is in Africa what is euphemistically known as 'informal governance' by international institutions, which has been intensified by the loss of sovereignty by African states due to the exigencies of structural adjustment. Key ministries have been literally hijacked by these institutions, placed out of the reach of domestic politics. Not surprisingly, given past practice, there is apprehension on the part of international financial institutions about democratic management of economic affairs. There is concern about public scrutiny of aid programmes and the behaviour of aid agencies. For the major financial institutions, their ideal remains that of a ministry of finance that is insulated from democratic processes and conducts 'policy dialogues' with the outside world unencumbered by domestic politics. Writing on one country whose performance has been widely hailed in the development establishment, Hutchful (1989) points to the erosion of national sovereignty, the 'depoliticisation' that has occurred, and the 'displacement of popular participation and mobilisation by a narrowly-based, bureaucratic management'. He argues:

> ...it is clear that there is a fundamental inconsistency between the market ideologies of the ERP/SAP and mass mobilisation, and between the highly secretive conditions of the programme's negotiations and the exercise of democratic participation. Ghana has been turned into a laboratory for extensive neo-classical experimentation, unencumbered by the distractions of popular democracy.

There is no need to belabour the point that such 'hijacking' of key elements of the state will conflict with the democratisation processes taking place in Africa. At best it will yield a highly truncated version of democracy by denying domestic political forces access to important spheres of national life. Experience from Latin America is enlightening. Writing on the case of Bolivia where a democratic regime has pursued a highly orthodox economic adjustment programme, Malloy (1991) notes that the reality of economic crisis and its attendant need to create an insulated, autonomous, decision-making capacity produces a strong authoritarian bent:

> What we see emerging in Latin America... is a new kind of regime that will not conform to pre-existing concepts of 'liberal democracy'. Rather we see a hybrid regime evolving in which an outward democratic form is energised by an inner authoritarian capacity especially in the realm of economic policy.

That donors in Africa aspire to this brand of truncated democracy is not a very far-fetched proposition. The preference for such an arrangement is so obvious to the new regimes that they tend to appoint technocrats from international organisations as prime ministers and finance ministers and seek to assure donors that these technocrats will be accorded autonomy in their management of the economy.

The Economic Interests of Donors

As far as the commitment to democratisation by donors in specific countries in Africa is concerned, this has already provoked serious disappointments in some parts of Africa. The British have tended not to take the matter seriously, confining themselves to 'quiet diplomacy' without much success.

France, which made a high-profile commitment to democratisation and distanced itself from authoritarian rule at the Baule meeting of June 1990, has raised the most expectations and provoked the most disappointment among the new leaders of democratic movements. Madagascar has made accusations against France for not disavowing Didier Ratsiraka and for not forcing him out of power; the Togolese, whose new Prime Minister invited French troops to dislodge the military supporters of Eyadema, were shocked to learn that the French troops who had moved to neighbouring Benin would only intervene to save French lives; and the Prime Minister of the transitional government of Congo was jolted to realise that France would not pick up the salary bill. A *Jeune Afrique* editorialist noted the ambivalence or even contradictory positions of the democratic movements which, while decrying France's constant interventions in their nations' affairs only yesterday, were now calling for French troops and the underwriting of budgets in a manner reminiscent of neocolonialism in its worst form. The editorialist went on to condemn these movements for the 'pernicious tendency, inherited from those against whom they have fought' to always turn to France.

These may be harsh words for embattled regimes such as that of Togo, but they raise a question which in some cases is leading to serious divisions among democratic movements themselves. The conflict arises from the difficulties of reconciling national sovereignty and the need for external support, even for such basic things as monitoring elections or keeping soldiers off the back of the new democracies. The case of Togo has dramatically dramatised this problem. The army's constant blackmailing of the new civilian regime there has tempted the opposition to call for France's intervention from its contingent in neighbouring Benin.

As for conflict of interests, it should be recalled that there are some powerful private economic interests in the donor countries which are closely tied to the predatory practices of the past and are understandably wary of the new democratic turn of events. These interests may enjoy enough political leverage or support to be able to exert sufficient pressure on their home governments to dilute their commitment to democratisation. The case of France in Gabon, Congo and Cameroon is suggestive of this phenomenon. It appears that ELF-Aquitaine, a major French oil company, has been involved in the disappearance of billions of dollars of oil revenue from these countries. Opposition movements in all of these countries have called for audits of the deals involving this company. This eventuality must have given French interests cold feet and may account for France opting for either cosmetic change, drawn-out processes of democratisation or even simply the status quo.

The Donors' Perception of Policy-making in Africa

Finally, the political conclusion that democratisation would be necessary or compatible with major economic programmes for African countries supported or imposed by both bilateral and multilateral donors contradicts the political analysis underlying the perception of economic policy by the donor community. To the extent that it is possible to impute an analytical framework to the World Bank's understanding of the politics of economic policy-making in Africa, one should note that this framework has changed over the years (Gibbon 1994). In the 1960s, the Bank tended to treat the state within a basically 'modernisation' paradigm, in which the state played an essentially benign, developmental role. And in any case, the Bank's confinement to projects did not necessitate a more complex view of the state than this. In the early 1980s, the view changed. Macroeconomic policies were then perceived as being so fundamentally misguided as to make any project financing meaningless. If projects were to be economically viable, macroeconomic policies had to be favourable. The Bank initially worked on the 'basket case' view that because African states were in dire straits, the Bank could introduce 'shock treatments' without much opposition from the recipient states. However, the reluctance of many states to accept the treatment and the recidivism of those who had accepted the package compelled the Bank towards some more explicit political analysis. It accepted the 'urban bias' thesis advanced by Michael Lipton to explain the persistence of poverty in the underdeveloped countries. With this thesis one could understand why it was politically rational to persist with what were obviously economically irrational policies. Politically, it opened up the vista for the Bank to seek out political coalitions that would be supportive of its policy recommendations.

Failure to identify, let alone constitute, such coalitions has forced the Bank to once again change the political-economy paradigm informing its understanding of political processes. The current view of the Bank is informed by a relatively new approach variously labelled 'rational choice', 'the public choice', the 'new political economy' or 'neo-classical political economy'. Developed by trade theorists to explain various protectionist policies that led to 'market distortion', the 'political economy of rent-seeking societies' posits interest groups that engage in 'Directly Unproductive' (DUP) activities to capture various rents generated by state activities. Common in all of these is a methodological approach which assumes rational individual behaviour in pursuance of self-interests as the cornerstone of political alliances and interest groups.

Intellectually, this political analysis carries the epistemological advantage of consistency and parsimony with respect to assumptions used since it merely extends to politics the methodological individualism and rationality derived from economic analysis. People maximise their utilities in politics just as they do in the market. This consistency and parsimony has, however, been gained at the cost of the empirical vacuity of assertions about how policy is actually made in Africa.

The salient point about this approach is that for policy analysis, the state is seen as essentially a rent-allocating agent. By definition, any involvement of the state in productive activities is simply an expression of its distributive functions. If it is involved in production at all, it is either to create employment for the bureaucracy or to facilitate the economic activities of certain interest groups, but not for economic growth. In either case, state activities create 'distortions' which lead to the loss of static allocative efficiency (while much has been blamed on these 'distortions', empirical measures of losses caused by them have turned up embarrassingly low figures). The political conclusion of this perspective is that good governance in the poor countries would require freeing the state from the demands of different domestic groups or, where this is not possible, a dramatic reduction of its role in the economy.

For a number of years, several North American scientists have used this approach to explain policy-making in Africa (Bates 1981; Rothchild and Curry 1978). Indeed, the plausibility of their explanation has been such that it has now entered the conventional consensus about politics and policy-making in Africa. What presumably makes matters worse in Africa is that the state (or, at least the 'State class') is itself a rent-seeker and a highly advantaged one at that.

There are at least three political problems with this interpretation of policy-making in Africa and elsewhere, for that matter. The first is that, pushed to its logical conclusion, it has a strong authoritarian predilection and anti-political penchant for it cannot relate to those activities that are inherent to democratic politics. Seeking as it does a state that is autonomous of various domestic interest groups, it is an analysis that admires the 'political will' of a militaristic Rawlings and condemns the lack of spine of those regimes which have to relate to a whole range of interests in an essentially political way. It is also a view that justifies extensive intervention of foreign institutions, which are putatively not implicated in the debilitating 'DUP' activities. A consistent pursuance of this approach will therefore tend toward a cynical view of and disdain or trivialisation of politics, which are treated as largely pathological (Beckman 1991; Grindle 1991). More precisely, it leads to the denigration of or, at least, attempts to circumvent the institutional arrangements and political processes that are central to liberal democracy. The reasoning is that if all the politically active and well-organised groups are involved in rent-seeking activities, it is necessary to either bring in foreign powers or to seek a domestic 'Leviathan' that transcends local politics. The next step is a negation of democratic politics.

The second problem with this perception is that the social groups that are now pushing for democratisation in Africa have usually occupied leading positions in the political 'demonology' of international financial institutions and have been considered to be the ones responsible for the disastrous policies pursued by African states since independence. Even more significant is that it is opposition to structural adjustment rather than support for it that has mobilised these social groups in their struggles for democratisation. In the words of Beckman (1991), 'it is resistance to SAP, not SAP itself, that breeds democratic forces. SAP can be credited with having contributed to this development, not because of liberalism but because of its authoritarianism'.

Now if such are the roots of democratic struggles and if such is the likely content of democratic programmes in Africa, it is not clear how the political ascendancy of this 'urban bias', 'labour aristocracy' or 'rent-seeking' coalition can be reconciled with the economic adjustment programmes. Either the material interests of this coalition have been wrongly identified with the pre-SAP policies and their control of state policies exaggerated, or the state is so autonomous of these rent-seeking groups or so beholden to foreign interests that local interest groups count for naught; or the 'rational choice' assumed to underlie policy-making is not as determinant as the theory suggests. It is only by accepting the last presupposition that one can justify the patrician calls by the donor community for the elites that have hitherto constituted the nefarious 'rent-seeking' coalitions to behave more disinterestedly and to thus countenance the sacrifice of some of their interests.

Even more confounding is the fact that among those countries which have received the highest accolades for being 'strong adjusters' in Africa, the majority have not needed democracy to introduce adjustment programmes, much to the Bank's satisfaction. Ghana, Nigeria and Malawi, to name only a few, are authoritarian regimes. Indeed, historically, the 'laboratory conditions' for neo-liberal economic policies was Pinochet's Chile where the 'Chicago Boys' could inflict 'shock treatments' without the encumbrance of interest groups or democratic politics.

To reconcile the imperatives of adjustment and the political exigencies of democratisation, there is now the presupposition that democracy can legitimise a set of policies that are admittedly unpopular. It can also improve governance which would presumably improve state capacity to implement adjustment programmes.

This is how the World Bank (1991) puts it:

> Democracies, conversely, could make reform more feasible in several ways. Political checks and balances, a free press, and open debate on the costs and benefits of government policy could give a wider public a stake in reform. The need to produce good results in order to be reelected could help, rather than hinder, economic change: it increases government's incentives to perform well and keeps predatory behaviour in check.

Of course all this does not prove that the policies adopted will or should be compatible to the SAP process unless one believes that free discussion, absence of corruption, and broad participation in policy-making will ineluctably lead to consensus around adjustment. This is the conclusion that a monistic view of politics leads to; since there is only one 'right' theory, there can be no scope for conflict on what is desirable for society (Amadeo and Banuri 1991). The World Bank (1991) is, to its credit, aware that this may not happen:

> Democratic governments are not necessarily more adept at managing reform either. Transitional democratic governments, perhaps because their political base is still fluid, appear to be particularly fluid... On the whole the democratic authoritarian distinction itself fails to explain adequately whether or not countries initiate reform, implement it effectively, or survive its political fall-out.

The Bank seems to accept the argument that democratic rule may have long-term growth and equity advantages over authoritarian rule:

> ...there is suggestive evidence that links features of democratic systems positively with overall aspects of development and welfare. A further result emerges from the empirical literature on the relation between economic performance and political system: by developing human resources and more particularly, by investing in education, countries have been found to strengthen the basis for open systems. Some studies suggest that for a given level of income, improvements in social indicators are associated with freedom and liberty (ibid.).

But there is a catch here. These advantages of democracy are a result of the pursuance of a whole range of policies that structural adjustment programmes scorn. The cuts in expenditure on social services which democracies need for political survival and for which they are lauded clearly suggest that structural adjustment and democratic rule are not easily reconcilable.

The third problem of the approach relates to the fact that it cannot accommodate or explain changes in policy. Since the rational behaviour of individuals pursuing self-interests inevitably leads to a specific set of policies, there are no endogenous forces that can be identified with an entirely different set of policies or that are capable of exerting policy in a direction that would not inevitably lead to another set of distortions. As Grindle (1991) notes:

> ...if one is locked into an ahistorical explanation of why things are the way they are and the notion that existing situations demonstrate an inevitable rationality, it is hard to envision how changes in such situations occur except through catastrophic events or the exogenous introduction of wise statesmen or technocrats who are above petty political rationality.

Conflict Between Formal and Substantive Demand

In much of Africa, the formal expression of demands for democratisation is multi-party democracy. However, as has been made clear during the numerous 'national conferences', the new movements also have substantive demands which reject structural adjustment or blame it for the decline in the material well-being of their countries. The widespread understanding of these movements is that the democratisation process will create the political foundations for addressing the substantive demands of the emergent democratic forces. Together with the call for democratic form, there are therefore demands against 'immiserisation'. Quite bluntly, these social forces expect some visible changes in their economic well-being, if not immediately after elections then surely soon after. However, in Africa as elsewhere, formal political reform has generally proved easier than substantive economic reform. Structural adjustment envisages a passage through 'a vale of tears' before settling on a course of sustained growth. Initially, the valley was thought to be narrow and swiftly traversed. Now it is widely admitted that it may be much wider, perhaps taking decades to cross. How does one ensure the coexistence of the economic trough and political liberty? How is the economic logic of structural adjustment to be reconciled to the political logic of democratisation? For economists the nemesis of intelligent policies, the ghost in the machine, is what is known as 'macroeconomic populism', which Dornbusch and Edwards (1990) disfavourably define as:

> ...a policy perspective on economic management which emphasises economic growth and income redistribution and de-emphasises the risks of inflation and deficit financing, external constraints and the reaction of economic agents to aggregate non-economic policies.

Pressures on the new democratic regimes to lean towards some kind of 'macropopulism' are enormous. So far, this has not taken place in Africa. Part of this prudency arises from the expectation on the part of the new governments that 'good behaviour' will be rewarded with an inflow of funds to cushion some of the social effects of adjustment and to stimulate growth and employment. It also stems in part from a genuine belief of the new democratic movements that technocratic solutions may be closer to the solution than the highly subjective and arbitrary decisions of their predecessors.

It has for years been conventional wisdom that orthodox political measures demand authoritarian rule. The removal of subsidies on goods and services consumed by supposedly strong interest groups (the urban population), and the removal of activities upon which certain groups have earned rents would require a strong state with the 'political will' or 'courage' to override popular pressures. Pinochet and the Chicago Boys are the almost legendary coupling of authoritarian rule and orthodox adjustment programmes. The link between popular demands for democracy and adjustment would, therefore, seem to fly in the face of historical experience. Adjustment programmes, to the extent that international financial institutions will not relent on getting their monies repaid, will pose severe strains on the new democratic regimes that may emerge from the present political impasse.

The problem is not confined to Africa. In Latin America the problem of 'debt and democracy' has been a major preoccupation of political and social movements (Stallings and Kaufman 1989). In Eastern Europe democratisation has had to confront the problems of a generalised decline in economic well-being during what is expected to be a transient phase of movement from central planning to market economies. Noting the 'exceptionally contradictory' process of democratisation in the Soviet Union, Gavriil Popov, an advocate of the free market, notes:

> I see the main problem in the relationship between, on the one hand, populism and, on the other, the tasks that must be carried out if the economy and society are to be transformed. Clearly, we could not have overthrown the powerful totalitarian system without the active participation of millions of ordinary people. But now we must create a society with a variety of different forms of ownership, including private property; and this will be a society of economic inequality. There will be contradictions between the policies leading to denationalisation, privatisation, and inequality on the one hand and, on the other, the populist character of the forces that were set in motion in order to achieve those aims. The masses long for fairness and economic equality. And the further the process of transformation goes, the more acute and the more glaring will be the gap, between those aspirations and economic realities.

The Question of National Sovereignty

Given the widespread corruption in Africa and the gross mismanagement that some of the economies have been subjected to, it is tempting to accept any 'benevolent' foreign intervention in the political affairs of African countries. The temptation is even greater when some of these regimes have been set up or bolstered by foreign powers that now advocate democratisation. And indeed a number of Africans have called upon foreign governments and international financial institutions to exert more financial pressure on African countries to move towards political reform or to even intervene military in defence of democratic change. It should, however, be clear that democratic governance in Africa will have to address itself to issues of sovereignty and the extent of foreign involvement in the day-to-day affairs of African countries. Foreign institutions will be fundamentally mistaken if they assume that the rejection of incumbent national governments and calls by nationals for solidarity in the form of 'political conditionality' are an option for foreign domination. If anything, the confrontation with the local states is likely to be a prelude to the confrontation with foreign powers as these continue to exercise powers outside the legally and democratically constituted institutions and to demand repayment of debts from countries which cannot account for where the monies went or seek to impose policies which hurt large sections of the population.

Conclusion

The quest for democracy that has swept across much of the world has not left Africa untouched. The one-party state is now a beleaguered colossus whose collapse has either taken place or is imminent. One-man rule is disappearing rapidly, sometimes terribly as in the case of Liberia and Somalia. Yet, all is not well. First, in a number of cases the concessions to democratic demands have been no more than window-dressing to outmanoeuvre opponents or to hoodwink international agencies who are increasingly demanding some forms of democratisation as a precondition for their financial support.

Second, the new democratic regimes are inheriting crisis-ridden economies and are being saddled with economic conditionalities that are placing severe strains on their political energies by undercutting their political base. Chances are that if the democratic movements pay the least attention to their domestic constituencies, they will not meet the stringent demands of their external constituencies — foreign financial institutions. They will soon be seen to be lacking, in the strange language of structural adjustment, the 'political will' to ride roughshod over popular demands.

The third cause for concern is that democratisation is taking place at a time when the sovereignty of African states has been gravely compromised. Adjustment has given foreign decision-makers political leverage that is not compatible with democratic practice. Democratisation in Africa risks obtaining foreign assistance that may eventually restrict its competence in both the economic and political spheres. The point here is not to deny foreign solidarity to democratic struggle in Africa, but to warn against 'political conditionality' that would dilute democracy by holding individual states to both economic and political ransom. But even more crucially it is to caution against the naive expectations of democratisation riding on the tanks or being shielded by the pockets of foreign powers. Processes of democratisation have been largely unleashed by internal forces against undemocratic rule, violation of human rights and gross mismanagement of resources by internal forces and the imposition of deflationary economic policies by outsiders. If the process is to be firmly anchored in African societies then we should insist that the initiative towards democratisation remain in the hands of domestic forces. External support that is an expression of solidarity, and not the usual meddlesome condescension, is most welcome.

A forth problem is the prevalence of a dogma that severely narrows the economic options and unwarrantably ties democratisation to one economic practice or model. In much of the discussion on the politics of adjustment it is simply assumed that the economic prescriptions of the World Bank, while painful, are the only way out. And so the debates evolve around how societies can be made to swallow this bitter but only known cure and still remain democratic. However, the obvious absence of any sustainable success after nearly a decade of 'adjustment', despite the Bank's feverish search for such cases, the unravelling of neo-liberalism in such countries as the United States of America and Great Britain, and the discrepancy between the historical experience of what are touted as 'successful market economies' such as Japan, South Korea and Taiwan and the diktats of structural adjustment, suggest that the perception of adjustment as the only cure has more to do with the tenacity of a misplaced abstraction or dogma than economic logic or historical evidence. In any case, the complete foreclosure of debate on such key issues as taxation, intratemporal and intertemporal distributional issues, and the protection or promotion of particular economic activities or markets does not augur well for democracy since it drastically reduces the range of issues upon which democratic governments can pronounce themselves. As Amadeo and Banuri (1991) note, the failure of the state does not derive from its refusal to adhere to a theoretical dogma. Rather,

> it derives, in the short run, from its abandonment of the goal of governance in favour of theoretical certitudes; and in the long run, from its inability or unwillingness to create or modify institutions to facilitate the management of conflicts which are forever changing in form and intensity.

---

* This paper was presented at the Seventh General Assembly of CODESRIA, and first published by the Macmillan Press Ltd. in 1994. CODESRIA acknowledges with thanks this reprint.

References

Amadeo, Edward and Bauri, Tarig, 1991, 'Policy, Governance and the Management of Conflict', in T. Bauri (ed.) *Economic Liberalisation: No Panacea,* Oxford, Clarendon Press.

Bates, R, 1981, *Markets and States in Tropical Africa: The Political Basis of Agricultural Policies,* Berkeley, University of California Press.

Beckman, B, 1991, 'Empowerment or Repression? The World Bank and the Politics of African Adjustment', *Africa Development,* Vol. XVI, No. 1.

Bienen, H, and J, Waterbury, 1989, 'The Political Economy of Privatisation in Developing Countries', *World Development,* Vol. 17, No. 5.

Bourgi, Albert and Casterna, Christian, 1991, *Le printemps de l'Afrique,* Paris, Hachette.

Bratton, M, and Rothchild, D, 1992, 'The Institutional Bases of Governance in Africa', in Goran Hyden and Michael Bratton (eds.), *Governance and Politics in Africa,* Boulder, Col., Lynne Rienner.

Buchanan, J, 1981, 'Rent Seeking and Profit-Seeking', in John Buchanan, D, Tollison, Gordon Tullock (eds.), *Toward a Theory of the Rent-Seeking Society,* College Station, Texas A&M University Press.

Campbell, Bonnie and Loxley, John, 1989, *Structural Adjustment in Africa,* London, Macmillan.

Chazan, Naomi, and Rothchild, Donald (eds.) 1987, *The Precarious Balance: State and Society in Africa,* Boulder, Col., Westview Press.

Colclough, Chistopher, and Manor, James, (eds.), 1991, *States or Markets: Neo-liberalism and the Development Policy Debate,* Oxford, Clarendon Press.

Diamond, L, 1989, 'Beyond Autocracy: Prospects for Democracy in Africa', paper presented at the Inaugural Seminar of the Governance in Africa Programme, Carter Centre, 17-18 February.

Dornbusch, R, and Edwards, S, 1990, 'Macroeconomic Populism', *Journal of Development Economics,* Vol. 32, Vol. 1.

Gibbons, Peter, 1994, 'Toward a Political Economy of the World Bank', in T. Mkandawire and A. Olukoshi (eds.), *Between Liberalisation and Repression: The Politics of Adjustment in Africa,* Dakar, CODESRIA.

Grindle, Merilee, 1991, 'The New Political Economy: Positive Economics and Negative Politics', in G. Meier (ed.), *Politics and Policy Making in Developing Countries: Perspectives on the New Political Economy,* San Francisco, ICS Press.

Hirschman, Albert, 1970, *Exit, Voice and Loyalty: Responses to Decline in Firms, Organisations and States,* Cambridge, Mass., Havard University Press.

Hutchful, E, 1989, 'From "Revolution" to Monetarism', The Economics and Politics of the Adjustment Programme in Ghana', in B. Campbell and J. Loxley, *Structural Adjustment in Africa,* London, Macmillan.

Hyden, G, 1980, *Beyond Ujama in Tanzania: Underdevelopment and an Uncaptured Peasantry*, Berkeley, University of California Press.

Krueger, Ann, 1974, 'The Political Economy of Rent-Seeking Society', *American Economic Review*, Vol. 64, No. 3.

Lal, Deepak, 1983, *The Poverty of 'Development Economics'*, London, Institute of Economic Affairs.

Malloy, J, 1991, 'Democracy, Economic Crisis and the Problem of Governance: The Case of Bolivia', *Studies in Comparative International Development*, Vol. 26, No.2.

Mamdani, M, Mkandawire, T, and Wamba-dia-Wamba, E, 1988, *Social Movements, Social Transformation and Democratisation in Africa*, CODESRIA *Working Paper*, No. 1.

Mbembe, Achille, 1989, 'Economic Liberalisation and the Post-Colonial African State', paper presented at the Inaugural Seminar of the Governance in Africa Programme, Carter Centre, 17-18 February.

Meier, Gerald (ed.), 1991, *Politics and Policy Making in Developing Counties: Perspectives on the New Political Economy*, San Francisco, ICS Press.

Mkandawire, T, and Olukoshi, A, (ed.) (forthcoming), *The Politics of Structural Adjustment in Africa*, Dakar, CODESRIA.

N'daki, Gregoire, 1991, 'Africa Centrale Transparence Petrolière', *Africa*, December.

Nyongo', Anyang' (ed.), 1987, *Popular Struggles for Democracy in Africa*, London, Zed Press.

Popov, Gavriil, 1990, 'Dangers of Democracy', *New York Review of Books*, 16 August, p. 27. Mr. Popov is the recently elected mayor of Moscow and the editor of the journal *Issues of Economics*.

Prebisch, Raul, 'Dialogue on Friedman and Hayek from the Stand-point of the Periphery', *CEPAL Review*, No. 15.

Rothchild, D, and Curry, R, 1978, *Scarcity, Choice and Public Policy in Middle Africa*, Berkeley, University of California Press.

Ruttan, Vernon, 1991, 'What Happened to Political Development?', *Economic Development and Cultural Change*, Vol. 39, No. 2.

Sklar, Richard, 1989, 'Perestroika Without Glasnost', paper presented at the Inaugural Seminar of the Governance in Africa Programme, Carter Centre, 17-18 February.

Sorensen, G, 1991, *Democracy, Dictatorship and Development*, London, Macmillan.

Stallings, Barbara and Kaufman, Robert (eds.), 1989, *Debt and Democracy in Latin America*, Boulder, Col., Westview Press.

World Bank, 1991, *World Development Report 1991*, Washington DC, World Bank.

7. The International Dimensions of the Democratisation Process in Africa

Eboe Hutchful

The transition to democracy in Africa is occurring in the context of simultaneous and multiple transitions in the global order:

- The first development is the disappearance of an alternative hegemonic order in the form of the Soviet Union and the socialist bloc;
- The second, which is the other side of the same coin, is the achievement by the United States of military hegemony at the same time as its economic decline becomes more and more apparent with the dismantling of the military economy;
- The third development takes the form of three closely related, if contradictory processes: the globalisation of the capitalist economy (accelerated by the removal of political barriers to capital expansion and rationalisation); the emergence at the same time of a tripolar economic dispensation (the EEC, the North American free trade area, and Japan and the Pacific Rim); and growing pressures to enhance competitive efficiency among the main capitalist powers.

These pressures are likely to grow as economic competition replaces the military competition of the Cold War period. For the first time in the twentieth century, market ideology and free trade have become an international orthodoxy. Globalisation and free-market orthodoxy have important implications for the economic options confronting democratic movements.

- Fourth, we see, paradoxically, the re-emergence, within and in spite of this globalisation process, of nationalism and ethnic and sectarian feeling as an international force. The reformation of states and reshaping of state boundaries in the former Soviet zone and Africa is in a manner reminiscent of the nineteenth century and the period of African decolonisation;
- Fifth, there is growing multilateralism via a reshaped United Nations dominated once again by America and the Western powers and endowed with a new philosophy of interventionism. An important aspect of this is the attempt to broker peace in conflict regions (South

Africa, Cambodia, the Middle East, El Salvador) less to promote genuine democratic change than to advance the *pax Americana*;
- Finally, there is the rise of social and democratic movements, and the consequent emergence of 'international civil society' — a proliferation of horizontal and relatively autonomous organisations, national and international in scope, cutting across state lines and by-passing, supplementing, monitoring and to some extent displacing structured relationships between states, and bearing an international morality distinct from that of states. Combined with developments in Africa itself, these multiple transformations are endowing the process of democratisation with considerate uncertainty and unpredictability.

Africa and the Global Movement for Democracy

While rooted in indigenous forces, the movement for democracy in Africa has nevertheless been profoundly influenced by some of these international developments and remains extremely vulnerable to international events. Indeed, any understanding of the process of democratisation in Africa must appreciate the many growth points of democracy on the continent, its interrelationship with democratic struggles in the global arena, and the essentially contested meanings of the concept of democracy itself.

The impact on Africa of the democratic movements in Eastern and Central Europe is sufficiently well-known not to require further discussion. By demonstrating that the most entrenched dictatorships can be overthrown by popular resistance and action, the democratic movements in Eastern Europe energised civil society in Africa in ways not seen since the independence struggles, and in the process also helped to give a 'liberal' shape to the continent's democratic movements. Most importantly, by lifting the dead weight of imperialism, 'perestroika' gave renewed effectivity to domestic political struggles, allowing a settling of scores between regimes and their increasingly recalcitrant societies.

On the other hand, sufficient attention has not been paid to the impact of Western democratic movements on these developments in Africa, in particular the extent to which the rise of social movements and the struggle to reshape democracy in the West has helped to place democracy on the global agenda and establish interconnections between movements for democracy in various parts of the world. Indeed, while the effect of Eastern Europe has been exemplary, that of the Western movements on Africa has been much more structural.

The influence of the struggle for democracy in the West has been understated in part because of the ideologically motivated pretence that the development of democracy in the West is 'complete' and that liberal democracies remain outside the democratic revolutions convulsing other parts of the world — and are indeed in a position to 'export' democracy to the rest of the world.

This is of course not entirely untrue. The meaning of democracy remains deeply contested in the West (Gillies and Schmidt forthcoming). Since the 1960s the dominant ideologies and institutions of democracy in leading Western societies, and the alliance of the state bureaucracy, military-industrial complex and establishment labour have been challenged by the emergence of a variety of popular movements and community organisations — feminists, gay rights activists, ecologists, abortion rights activists, church groups and community rights movements.

These organisations worked outside, and often against, the established institutions of democracy and the traditional areas of control of the power elite. The significance of these movements resides in their alternative, participatory vision of democracy. As opposed to the episodic voting or competition for state power prescribed by 'elite' democracy, the social movements in the West have been concerned with 'empowerment', in other words with creating an environment in which ordinary people, groups and organisations could exercise control over or the decisions affecting their lives, particularly at the community level.

Existing forms of democracy, with their opaque processes of decision-making, disempower rather than empower the mass of ordinary citizens. The political skill of these movements has been reflected in their understanding of the public policy process and in the use of sophisticated organisational, research, public policy and judicial techniques, largely exploiting openings made available by the state itself. In the domestic and sometimes international arena these movements have challenged the agenda of the state in the areas of ecology, reproductive and gender rights, poverty and human rights, sometimes on the basis of their own autonomous international networks.

However, these movements have not attempted to challenge the state or its basic legitimacy, only its way of doing business. Essentially middle class and professional rather than working class in origin, they have not sought to capture power as such nor to transform existing political structures (although their attempts to form coalitions and to interconnect issues could lead them occasionally in the direction of an anti-systemic critique), but to ensure participation, accountability and equity. Indeed, their greatest strength has been in the ways in which they used existing freedoms to mobilise around specific issues, thus radically expanding the horizons of democratic participation.

Although basically committed to democratic practices, these social movements were seen as a threat to the existing forms of 'elite' or 'polyarchial' democracy. In the early 1970s conservatives were warning of a 'governability crisis' as a result of their activities (Crozier 1975; Offe 1984).

Despite the frequently confrontational character of these movements the capitalist state sought in many cases to accommodate or incorporate them, even providing a platform for them (administrative hearings, judicial processes, etc.). Where an accommodation has been reached with the state, their collaboration in effect has greatly extended the social and international penetration of the state. What has emerged in effect is a new type of expanded corporatism which has implications not only for the democratic structure at home but also for international relations and for the practice of development.

To reach their international goals most of these movements have found it necessary to gain access to the funding and international access controlled by the Western state and aid bureaucracies. As 'development practitioners' they had considerable influence on the way development is conceived and implemented. In return the development bureaucracies have been able to use the organisations to legitimise their programmes and penetrate areas that governmental organisations (with their known political coloration) may not have been able to reach. Thus tied in complex ways to the state and bureaucracy, these movements have sometimes helped to carry forward the international agenda of the Western state and development bureaucracies on the basis of mutual concerns.

This increasing interpenetration of state organisations and these organisations and movements reminds one of Gramsci's (1971) formulation regarding civil society in the advanced capitalist democracies.[1] The collaboration, however, is always a critical one, and ensures some degree of accountability of the development bureaucracies to national constituencies.

Western social movements have been responsible to a large degree for putting such issues as gender, ecology and human rights on the international agenda and for monitoring governmental action or inaction in these areas. They have been able to use the relative political freedoms in their own countries to address issues which social movements in authoritarian regimes may not have been able to pursue. It is in this sense of creating a common international morality autonomous of (and sometimes even hostile to) states and linking social and political struggles that one may speak of the beginnings of an international civil society.

Because of their specific national and political situations and philosophies, social movements in different parts of the world stand to contribute differently (both in terms of process and content) to the formation of the global civil society. The specific contribution of Western social movements, implicating their national states, has had both positive and negative implications for democratic developments in Africa.

The Concepts of Democracy

The conjoint but separable interests[2] of the Western state, development bureaucracies and the Western non-government organisations/social movements[3] have resulted in at least two distinct and conflicting but at the same time overlapping notions of democracy being pursued in Africa.

The first concept may be described as 'formal democracy'. This identifies democracy with free and periodic elections, a multi-party system, a free press and judiciary, the rule of law and other liberal democratic rights and freedoms. This is the version of democracy advocated by Western governments and increasingly being enforced through political conditionality. 'Democracy' is related to 'development' in the sense that the 'free individual' and free markets are seen as the basis of development. 'Democracy' thus becomes necessary for 'development', and the lack of 'development' in Africa is blamed on the failure of African regimes to adopt 'democracy".

The second is the notion of 'empowerment' associated with Western NGOs, development agencies and donor organisations, and more recently the World Bank. Unlike formal democracy, empowerment is not associated with the existence of particular political institutions and/or rights but defined in terms of the ability of community associations, interest groups and other organisations to participate in and influence the decisions that affect their lives, as well as the creation of an environment that facilitates such outcomes.

Empowerment is defined less in terms of the overall political context than of specific policy processes. The advantage of this concept is that—unlike 'democracy' — it is considered to be less ethnocentric, or tied to particular political structures and institutions. And, unlike liberal democracy, 'empowerment' is more oriented to 'micro' community and marginal groups, and emphasises the group (rather than individual) and direct (rather than indirect) participation. Nevertheless, the concept of 'empowerment' is used in a variety of senses, radical as well as conservative. The right-wing versions tend to see empowerment in terms of the enhancement of market choices and accountability to market actors. This is the version encountered in the World Bank's 1989 report on Africa. Like formal democracy, empowerment is considered necessary for 'development', not in the sense of accumulation and the activities of the freely investing entrepreneur (although this version is strong in the World Bank's concept) but in terms of the satisfaction of basic needs. Ultimately, however, all groups in society can be 'empowered' (and need to be if the system is to work properly).

Though controversial, political conditionality has nevertheless given impetus to democratic transition in Africa by forcing recalcitrant regimes to yield to demands for competitive politics and human rights. Nevertheless, in its ethnocentric and ideological form it carries the danger of pre-empting distinctive local versions of democracy. As pushed by Western governments, 'democracy' virtually ignores issues of social and economic justice in Africa and the global system, and appears as a barely concealed post-Cold War formula for American and Western strategic and economic interests.

In particular, American commitment to democracy appears selective and manipulative. Human Rights Watch rightly attacked the Bush Administration for defending human rights 'only when it is cost-free' and for misusing the State Department's Bureau for Human Rights and Humanitarian Affairs to defend abusive governments. Although American pressures for democratisation have leaned heavily on lavish promises of financial aid, the results for regimes which have been taken in by these promises have been almost laughable.[4]

On the other hand, the empowerment approach, by laying emphasis on participation in sector policy processes and projects and specialised, micro-level action by affected groups, rather than on broad political processes and alliances, encourages particularistic and fragmented levels of action. As used in development circles, empowerment is developmentalist, functionalist and basically apolitical, partly as a matter of principle (many of those using this terminology are aid bureaucrats for whom the term is appealing because it avoids issues of politics), and partly out of a sense of realism (to protect the privileged access enjoyed by these organisations). This approach favours working indirectly to strengthen the institutions of civil society while ignoring those of political society. A further weakness of the concept (particularly in its conservative usage) is a tendency to focus almost entirely on the way in which the state and formal political authorities work to disempower groups in society, ignoring social contradictions and sources of oppression.

This apolitical, piecemeal 'community-based' approach in effect strengthens the state at the margins, either by encouraging community groups to pick up the slack through 'self-help' as the state retrenches, or by emphasising a 'developmental partnership' in which the state is essentially legitimised through its role as senior partner. Official recognition, while involving clear advantages (including the ability to function at all), may compromise the autonomy of existing organisations by drawing them into the ambit of the state. By intervening in donor resource flows and inserting themselves between donors and NGOs (under the pretext of protecting the national interest or exercising supervision), governments are able to capture or assert control over community organisations, using these resources as bait to foster corporatist relationships. Organisations that insist on autonomy and accountability to their membership are those most likely to be excluded.

In addition, by imposing onerous controls on the operations and systems of financial accounting of the organisation, the donor organisation or international NGO may actually weaken accountability of leaders to the membership, redirecting such accountability to the donor organisation. We may then witness the development of a system of parallel governance, with control over the affairs of the organisation exercised simultaneously by the donor organisation at the one level and the national government at another.

Another effect of the complex system of controls and interventions exercised by external agencies is that cadres as well as members of the target organisation may feel a growing loss of control over the direction of the organisation (i.e., be disempowered) while in a technical sense proving 'successful' in attaining formal organisational objectives. Yet another consequence is a growing hierarchy and differentiation of civil organisations through selective NGO-isation. This involves processes of:

(a) bureaucratisation (the increasing operation of previously informal community organisations through bureaucratic methods);

(b) encadrement (professional interlocutors with grant application and administration skills);

(c) tutelage (by international organisations, often with unassimilable skills);

(d) dollarisation (orientation to the dollar as the basic unit of consumption and account); and

(e) 'officialisation' (recognition by the state).

Thus we can see from this analysis that problems arise with the tactics and political orientation of Western social movements when extended to movements in the Third World. Here the basic framework of rights and accountability do not exist and cannot be attained without confronting the state and transforming its fundamental character. A condition for these movements/NGOs being incorporated into official development networks and for being allowed to operate in the host country is their avowedly non-political character. Hence indigenous NGOs and social movements have been encouraged to see 'empowerment' in a depoliticised context.

Essentially because of their own political background and the circumstances of their work, many such organisations are driven to seek 'critical collaboration' relationships with the state which would promote 'accountability' (in a rather narrow sense) regardless of the specific form of the regime; hence they had difficulty working with indigenous social movements with broad political objectives (in particular labour has often been ignored).

The problem is partly social and partly contextual; unlike the social movements in the West, those in the Third World are led by genuinely grass-roots leaders, and in any case in the circumstances of the Third World many of the movements that would correspond to 'social movements' — as opposed to project-oriented NGOs — in the Western sense cannot operate without being 'political', and directly or indirectly advocating systemic change.

Thus, at least in Africa, because of the influence of these development organisations, as much as the lack of interest of Western governments, it was not until the collapse of the dictatorships in Eastern Europe that the issue became redefined in terms of 'democracy' — in other words, of the transformation of the basic political structures. The democratic movements and NGOs have emerged as separate and potentially hostile organisations. Partly as a consequence there has been a problem in articulating the apolitical 'social movement' view of democracy with the political view of democracy. Empowerment in the West occurred within certain (formally democratic) political structures; in Africa on the other hand 'empowerment' and 'democracy' have often carried different connotations, the former suggesting participatory development and the latter participatory politics. Initiatives for 'empowerment' have been carried on outside the context of political struggle. Not surprisingly, civil society and political society have appeared to be in conflict.

Most democratic movements in Africa have concerned themselves almost entirely with establishing the institutions of political society (in particular the political party and the electoral regime) rather than those of civil society; ignoring the political, administrative and legal environment necessary to allow community organisations and other special interest groups to operate effectively and autonomously. In return many NGOs and social movements have often been sceptical if not hostile to political parties claiming to represent democracy.[5]

However, even in the Western democracies the social movements have suffered multiple defeats, although registering significant impact in areas like the environment and reproductive rights. The emergence of Reaganism and Thatcherism demonstrated how little the movements had succeeded in transforming the basic institutions of capitalism and the workplace.

The reasons for these defeats are varied. The first is the basic character of liberalism and the inherent limits it places on those movements which accept its logic of participation. This is reflected in the way in which these social movements have conceptualised their own agenda, in particular their separation of political from economic struggles and specifically their self-distancing from working-class struggles. Given the nature of liberal fragmentation and the individualism of these movements, it is also not surprising that they have failed to maintain the unity of civil society against the state.

Almost invariably the rise of progressive organisations (such as the pro-choice movement) has precipitated a response in the rise of reactionary counter-movements. Ironically, the socio-political activation and fragmentation of civil society has resulted in greater arbitrative power of the state relative to civil society and intervention in its affairs, as well as the growing power and influence of the judiciary, the least politically accountable organ of the state.

Also important is the way in which the capitalist state has responded to these movements. While prepared to incorporate these movements into some policy organs it effectively excluded them from key institutions and policy processes of the state, such as economic and fiscal policy and defence and national security. Bureaucratic red-tape and non-performance frustrated advances made on the legislative front in areas like the environment. Deregulation placed market dynamics even further beyond their reach and control. New issues (such as globalisation) are arising within the capitalist economy to which these movements have no effective response.

Thus the notion that 'articulated democratic struggles' conducted by these middle-class movements in the singular would transform the structure of capitalism have been demonstrated to be premature and naive. Today the United States — the leading example of this form of democracy — appears less and less worthy of emulation. The unions have been silenced, tax policies have impoverished the middle class and poor alike while the rich become richer, unemployment and homelessness have increased sharply (incorporating strata of the population that would have been unimaginable only a few years ago), and fully 35 million Americans are without medical insurance of any kind. The state at all levels seems to be involved in a war against the poor and homeless, and inner-city violence has reached frightening new proportions. Fewer and fewer are deceived that this represents 'democracy' in any meaningful sense; it is no wonder that the National Organisation for Women recently demanded a new political force to 'ignite in the United States the revolution for democracy that is now sweeping the world'.

This defeat is not a local event, but international in scope; Western 'progressives' have also been powerless to prevent the emergence of rapidly free-market regimes following the democratic revolutions in the Soviet Union and Eastern Europe which they worked to foster. There is no guarantee against a similar outcome in Africa.[6]

The Africanist Contribution

Africanist social science has made a major contribution to the epistemologies underlying the current understanding of African problems and indirectly to the demand by foreign donors and development agencies for political change in Africa. From the early or mid-1980s (in particular following the publication of the Berg Report), a consensus emerged among certain Africanist circles, particularly in the United States, that Africa's problems were fundamentally political and domestic rather than economic or external in origin. The problem was identified as the continent's mode of governance.

One may categorise two major theoretical approaches or schools that influenced the debate. The first might loosely be termed the 'state realist school'. This school starts from the premise, based on the experience of the Newly Industrialising Countries (NICs), that the quality of state policy and leadership is the most crucial determinant of the success or failure of developing societies in transforming their global environment. It sees state weakness and the inability of the African state to 'get politics right' as the main cause of Africa's current crisis and of the social and economic decline of the continent relative to other Third World regions. For this it blames not only bureaucratic incompetence and political corruption but also the 'unruly diversity' and 'incaptured' character of Africa's 'precapitalist' social formations. It sees overcoming state recession and recovering state centrality and effectiveness as the key issue; in its view the solution is to 'harden' the state and strengthen its autonomy.

To these state realists liberal political models are not necessarily appropriate; indeed, the models used (the Asian and Latin American NICs) were anything but liberal in their politics. In at least one sense—its concern with political efficiency rather than rights—this school can be described as political neo-classicism.[7] At the same time it was pessimistic as to what was politically feasible in Africa.[8] 'Democracy' was not on the whole among the options considered (except perhaps as a strategic necessity); on the contrary, democracy was sometimes opposed on the grounds that it might further compromise state autonomy and effectiveness.

Opposed to the state realists is what I have sometimes called the 'school of sociality'. In this school may be included those Africanists who see African social networks as durable and flourishing under and in defiance of political authoritarianism and state crisis. While the state realists regard the diversity and myriad networks of African society as sapping at the 'soft underbelly' of the state, the sociality school looks to the solidarity and redistributionism of African society as providing the basis for social and community survival and renewal. State weakness presents a 'window of opportunity' for autonomising civil society and deepening and enriching social exchanges, particularly for marginal groups (women, informal sector operatives, rural poor, etc.) which stand outside the state and privileged formal networks. The solution is to turn away from the politics of the state to the politics of community.

Thus while the state realists are characterised by political pessimism, this second school is typified by social optimism, and social diversity is healthy and should be encouraged. Nevertheless, while definitely more libertarian (or communitarian) in sentiment than the state realists, this school does not explicitly see the solution in terms of democracy either. Neither does it contemplate political action to capture the state. Both schools were suspicious of politics but from very different angles: one wary of the state and its impositions, the other of the fractious community that weakens the state. Here, in thin disguise, was the familiar debate between the 'governability' and the 'social movements' schools in the United States.

'Socialism' and 'Democracy' in the 'New World Order'

The collapse of state socialism in the Soviet Union and Eastern Europe has been central to the emergence and victory of the democratic movements in Africa. Does this mean that 'socialism' is forever dead and that 'democracy' (presumably in its liberal form) is triumphant? This question requires a realistic appraisal of the political terrain that has emerged from the ashes of the Cold War:

- The 'New World Order', first, has produced not only democracy, but also new fundamentalisms — nationalist, religious, fascist and racist;

- Second, it has confirmed the apparent victory of market ideologies that emphasise economic efficiency regardless of social and political cost, while at the same time de-emphasising issues of justice and the restructuring of the global economy. This is the new economic fundamentalism;

- Third, the collapse of the 'Soviet Empire' is too often seen by Western officialdom (particularly in the United States) in terms of the renewed march of an imperialistic liberalism, only temporarily interrupted by the events of 1917.

The problem with this latter view is (or should be) already apparent. What has occurred is not the final triumph of liberal reason and the 'end of history'. Rather it is the liberation of many local and national histories subordinated by the dynamics of imperialism. Liberalism has effected the defeat of official socialism only to encounter new/old centres of resistance to liberal reason, much more stubborn, elusive and 'irrational', in the resurgence of nationalism and religious fundamentalism. Instead of one Soviet Union, many potential Yugoslavias, Somalias and Iraqs.

In retrospect, by organising the world behind two rival hegemonies the Cold War actually simplified the terrain of global struggle and the strategic agenda of liberalism. Liberalism and socialism at least share a common language: they are both Eurocentric in origin and in aspiration universalistic, modernist and humanist. Today liberalism encounters not a rival hegemonic discourse of universal reason but many dispersed centres of political autonomy and initiative based on the rediscovery of previously submerged cultures and national aspirations and animosities— societies for which the clock of history has been rewound. To the extent that this 'atavism' and fragmentation are the result in part of the denial by state socialism of national aspirations and cultural, religious and ideological diversity; it contains a powerful warning for liberal chauvinism also.

Further, the collapse of official socialism is unlikely to presage the end of socialism as such. The diversity of historical sources of socialism indicates that socialism corresponds to deeply held human and ethical values. What differed — and herein lay the differences in scope of the various traditions of socialism—were the strategies for articulating and achieving these values according to historical, national and class circumstances. If anything, the demise of state socialism will lay bare the rich and authentic tradition of socialistic values, no less real for the fact that they may no longer answer to the same nomenclature. The basic ideas and aspirations of socialism (although perhaps no longer existing as an autonomous discourse) will almost certainly be restated as an integral part of the struggle for democracy and of democratic discourse itself. The same old questions will continue to be posed, but within the framework of democracy.

The Cold War had inspired a double mystification: that on the one hand the Soviet Union represented 'socialism' while America on the other stood for 'democracy'. In this sense the abolition of socialism as an autonomous discourse will facilitate the rearticulation of the struggle for socialism and democracy, abolishing 'democracy' in turn as an autonomous discourse of formal rights and structures.

Thus not 'democracy', but 'what kind of democracy'? will be the pertinent question of the future. The insistence on the unitary nature of democracy (equated with 'liberal democracy') and on a 'democracy without prefixes' is an attempt to pre-empt this debate over the real meaning of democracy.[9] On the other hand, liberalism has established an irrefutable claim to a fragment of the democratic experience. The value of liberal notions of formal rights can no longer be denied.[10] However, as long as there are other rights intrinsic to the democratic experience which liberalism denies, the notion that liberalism constitutes in any sense the 'completion' of democracy should be resisted. A holistic definition of democracy must both incorporate and transcend the liberal concept of rights.

Relations with the Former Soviet Zone

A key question facing the global movement for democracy is the kind of relationships that will emerge between Africa and the former zone of socialism, in particular the degree to which alliances can be forged between the democratic movements in the two regions. Such alliances on the international scene could consolidate transnational civil society against the power of states, while at home and abroad protect against reversion to authoritarianism and imperialism. It is as yet unclear what forms the new relationships might take. What is clear is that the demise of the Soviet bloc has deprived African countries of the latitude (diplomatic, political and military) in international politics that they had enjoyed with the Cold War.

Conversely, the historical relationship between Africa and the old Soviet Union had probably run its logical course and become progressively counter-productive for both parties. Since the 1960s Soviet aid to Africa had declined in diversity, scope and depth; in many respects (other than the military) the Soviet Union was in danger of becoming irrelevant in Africa. From the historical standpoint also the relationships established by the Soviets with Africa appear in retrospect remarkably shallow. This relationship was overwhelmingly between states, hardly ever penetrating or involving the civil societies.

This is one of the key difficulties faced by new regimes in the two regions as they attempt to forge new relationships. This limitation was inherent in the nature of the relationship conducted by the Soviet Union as a state socialist regime and could not be transformed or transcended without fundamental changes in the nature of that state. Reform in the former Soviet bloc raises at least the theoretical possibility that a new form of relationship involving more diverse interactions, interests and actors may now be possible.

While the nature of the democratic movements in the former socialist zone may be problematic, there seem two obvious difficulties in the way of such a relationship:

- The first is the political isolationism and the xenophobic nationalism that has emerged among the republics, in clear opposition to the internationalism of the former Soviet state. In particular, interest in Third World affairs has fallen sharply since 'perestroika', and on the

international scene the new regimes have shown little interest in identifying with Third World causes;
- Second, unlike Africa, the democratic intelligentsia in the region is wedded to an extreme version of free marketism which may be difficult in practice to reconcile with its democratic aspirations. Given the shallow roots of democratic culture in the region, the strength of right-wing nationalist and fundamentalist forces, and the shock of the transition to free markets, the outcome for democracy in many of the former socialist countries is far from assured.

Many of these problems must obviously be seen as transitional difficulties and overreactions to the excesses of the former regimes. Hopefully, as democratic forces mature in the region they may have much of value to exchange with Africa in the area of consolidating democracy in multi-ethnic societies.

At the economic level similar problems of reinsertion into the global economy may provide a new basis for solidarity between the two regions. The new states of Eastern and Central Europe may be important allies in the reform of the multilateral banks and the new international economic order; in theory their membership in the IMF and the World Bank should result in a major redistribution of power in those institutions.[11] It is also possible that the republics may open up important new markets for African merchandise with liberalisation and economic recovery.

Unfortunately, African concerns have focused less on these positive possibilities than on the consequences of aid diversion to the region; the possible effects of renegotiation of the former Soviet and Eastern European debts on financial markets and Third World debt-rescheduling; the disruption of commodity markets from dumping (particularly of gold and diamonds) by Russia; and the possibility of Eastern and Central Europe emerging as the new 'Third World' of the EEC and the West.[12]

Democracy in an Age of Market Fetishism

More important than any economic competition between Africa and the former Soviet bloc is the common danger faced by democratic transitions in both regions from the global economic situation. At the same time as democracy has been placed on the agenda, talk of reforming the global economic order has receded. Aid flows have stagnated or diminished.

In addition, the G7 group of industrial countries increasingly monopolises discussion of key economic issues. This is not accidental, as a study of the literature should make clear. As the emphasis in the development literature has shifted from external to domestic and political factors, political and policy reform (good governance and adjustment), not restructuring the global economic system, are seen as the solution.

In many influential quarters democracy is viewed as a substitute for, not a complement to, the reorganisation of the international economic order. Countries in economic distress are asked to adopt 'democracy' and 'free markets'. In this situation both Africa and the former Soviet bloc can look forward for the foreseeable future to a global economy characterised by unstable and declining commodity prices, through conditionality, capital export and discriminatory debt treatment.

One of the myths of the new economic fundamentalism that today dominates the international discourse on development is the natural compatibility of democracy and the market. Donor countries see market-oriented reform and democratisation as parallel processes and are insisting that the two go together.[13] This notion of the necessary harmony of markets and democracy, far from being an orthodox wisdom of liberal democracy, is on the contrary a transparent (and fairly recent) piece of revisionism.

Both, Macpherson (1973) and John Stuart Mill before him, have argued convincingly that capitalism and democracy belong to different genealogies and structural logics, and require to be brought consciously into some compatibility with each other. By the end of the Great Depression virtually all leading capitalist democracies concurred to some degree with this view. Sustaining democracy required some state intervention into markets; in Europe social democratic parties initiated measures to engineer a fragile consensus between market dynamics and democratic rights and stability. With the possible exception of the United States, all mature capitalist democracies are highly managed economies; none correspond to the 'free markets' envisaged in the World Bank literature.

With the fiscal crisis of the welfare state, however, the question of the tension between 'democracy' and market efficiency resurfaced. As right-wing as well as social democratic regimes turned to the market, the 'enterprise culture' required to regenerate economic growth in the 1980s was seen as incompatible with the mechanisms that had been used to engineer democratic consensus since the end of the Second World War.[14]

At the global level this economic fundamentalism represents probably a greater threat to democracy than any of the other fundamentalisms— and we are not just referring to the NICs. The threat posed by this 'shock therapy' for democratic transitions is too often recognised to require further mention; even before the introduction of the Russian market reforms the (former) Mayor of Moscow and a stalwart of the democratic movement, Gavril

Popov, was warning of the 'dangers of democracy' and arguing the need to curb democracy to allow the introduction of market reforms.

In Africa, where democratic movements are not as wedded to free-market ideology, the tests are going to be yet greater. This should not by any means be construed as an argument against economic efficiency; we now know well enough that no democracy will survive without a solid economic foundation. What is false is the notion that economic efficiency demands the shredding of the social compact and the expulsion of the state from the economy.

On the contrary, it is those capitalist countries that have maintained a strong social compact and the vigorous participation of the state in the economy (such as Japan) that have registered the highest competitiveness and growth, while those who have sought to maintain classic 'free markets' (such as the United States) have declined.

This said, however, both globalisation and free-market orthodoxy are fundamentally altering the economic terrain of democratic struggles. The notion that the economy lies 'beyond politics' seeks consciously to place economic issues outside democratic struggles. On the other hand, globalisation suggests that an economic strategy for the consolidation of democracy can no longer be formulated on a purely national basis.

What is required is interconnection of democratic struggles on a global basis. This will not be easy, considering that globalisation carries very different implications for national economies and individual democratic movements. However, democracy cannot long survive if states beggar their populations and their neighbours in order to attract capital. As a global event democracy can be sustained only if it is built on national and international equity — on a foundation that recognises the economic needs and rights of all peoples and nations — and for this conscious agreement between democratic movements on the rules of the economic game is necessary.

Notes

1. In Canada, one of the best examples of this form of collaboration, the number of NGOs funded by CIDA, the federal development agency, grew from 20 (about 2% of the CIDA budget in 1968) to about 200 (8.3% of the total budget) in 1983. John S, Clark, 'Canadian Non-Government Organisations and their Influence on Canadian Development Policy', University of Toronto, Development Studies Programme, Working Paper No. A17, October 1985. Clark argues that CIDA's actions are 'not motivated entirely by philosophy', and that 'by funding NGOs CIDA sought to boost public support for its own overseas projects...[and] unite these NGO constituencies behind Ottawa's foreign aid policies'. It must be stressed that the level of collaboration with NGOs differs from state to state. It

is relatively low in the United States, in part because of the national security concerns underlying much US aid abroad.

2. In this discussion of CIDA and the NGOs, Clark (*ibid.*) argues that the '[Canadian] federal government and the NGO community have fairly different notions of what development is, and how to go about obtaining it... Because of these differences, there are instances where an NGO's work in a country may be hindered by the policies of CIDA, External Affairs, or other government department...'

3. An objection may be made in the discussion that follows that it appears to collapse 'social movements' and NGOs. Social movements are, in a technical sense, 'non-governmental organisations'. However not all NGOs can be considered social movements. Social movements unite a board membership for common action in the pursuit of social objectives and are (at least in theory) accountable to that membership. While many 'NGOs' answer to this description (and indeed on the international scene many NGOs are organisational extensions of Western social movements) many NGOs active in the development field have no |membership' to speak of and offer specialised services (including that of monitoring government agencies) on the basis of government o voluntary funding, often working through indigenous organisations in their areas of operation. What is important in the relationship that I am trying to draw here is that many Western (or 'international') NGOs are purveyors of ideas popularised by social movements at home. It is this philosophical identity that is important. (Again, as we saw in the example of CIDA, by working through the NGOs the development agencies assure some degree of accountability to and support from domestic social movements). In the Third World the distinction is more fundamental. Here the term 'NGO' can carry specific connotations (see the discussion below), and does not cover all organisations operating outside the governmental sector (indeed one of the distinguishing characteristics of NGOs in popular parlance is their connection to official or semi-official agencies. In Africa at least, an 'NGO' is an organisation that aspires to be included in international development networks!). Some organisations are established right from the start as 'NGOs', while others (already existing organisations) become 'NGOs' (again see the discussion below).

4. When the Baltic states became independent after 50 years of American pressure, the Bush administration congratulated them by giving them $14 million. But after Panama succumbed to the US invasion, President Elderet had to go on a hunger strike to obtain even a fraction of the aid promised for collaborating with the United States. And after many years of war in Nicaragua (with lavish aid of the contras) Chamorro was pointedly ignored when she arrived in Washington to claim the aid promised as a condition for defeating the Sandinistas (Greenberger 1991).

5. In both Ghana and Nigeria this hostility was most apparent among the NGOs well connected with the existing government and donor agencies. What was striking on the whole was the indifference toward questions of democracy.

6. In a recent report, Human Rights Watch has warned against the danger of 'token electoralism' emerging on the continent, including in countries such as Nigeria.
7. On the other hand, few members of this school support the World Bank's insistence on strong state as necessary for economic success (Hyden 1983, Sandbrook 1985, Price 1984, Ergas 1986).
8. Thus Sandbrook advocates 'benevolent patrimonialism', Hyden the take-over of power by the entrepreneurial bourgeoisie, and Ergas the extension to Africa of the Latin American bureaucratic-authoritarian regime.
9. An example of the regrettable efforts in this direction is the extraordinarily narrow definition of 'democracy' advanced in the four-volume work.
10. This is a lesson that the democratic movements in Africa have learned well. See the discussion on Ghana in my paper 'Shades of Meaning: The Struggle to Define Democracy in Ghana', conference paper, Canadian Association of African Studies Annual Conference, York University, Toronto, May 1991.
11. On the other hand, it is far from clear that this redistribution of power will necessarily work in the interest of the Third World. In conversations with scholars from the former Soviet Union there seems to be a consensus that the new regimes in the region will not necessarily support G77 positions on such issues as Third World debt and market-oriented adjustment.
12. It is possible that such fears (while not unreasonable) are somewhat exaggerated. As I have argued elsewhere, both aid and foreign direct investment have been slow to materialise in Eastern and Central Europe, and the argument does not take into account the de facto debt-relief that inability to collect former Soviet and Eastern European credits will afford many of the most distressed Third World countries (with outstanding loans of 94.3 billion roubies the Soviet Union is a *net creditor* by some margin). In addition, I suggest that African countries may not be much less competitive that the poorer former Soviet Republics.
13. This has become the source not only of the new dictatorship (you must have both 'democracy' and free markets) but also of censorship. When a commissioned study on democratic development cited potential conflicts between adjustment and the democratisation process (even though generally supporting the argument regarding the compatibility of markets and democracy) a national aid agency ordered the offending passages removed or toned down.
14. See 'No Return to Corporations, Days 21', *Financial Times*, 31 December 1990, 31, formerly Investors in Industry, is a British Industrial conglomerate.

References

Calaghy, Thomas, 1989, *Beyond Autocracy in Africa* (a collection of papers from a seminar held under the Governance in Africa Program of Carter Centre of Emory University, Atlanta, in February 1989), p.96.

Chazan, Naomi, 1983, *An Anatomy of Ghanaian Politics: Managing Political Recession,* Westview and essays by Mc Gaffey and others in Nzongola-Ntalaja, The Crisis in Zaire: Myths and Realities.

Clark, John, S, 1985, 'Canadian Non Government Organisations and their Influence on Canadian Development Policy', University of Toronto, Development Studies Programme, Working Paper No. A17, October.

Crozier, Michael *et al.*, 1975, The Crisis of Democracy, Report on the Governability of Democracies to the Trilateral Commission, New York, New York University Press. For a general discussion and critique of such positions, see Offe, Claus, 1984, 'Ungovernability: The Renaissance of Conservative Theories of Crisis', in Claus Offe, Contradictions of the Welfare State, London, Hutchison and Co.

Detroit Free Press, 1991, September 9, p.1.

Detroit Free Press, 1991, December 30, p.1.

Diamond, Larry, Linz Juan et Lipset Seymour Martin (eds.), 1988, *Democracy in Developing Countries,* Boulder, Lynne Rienner Publishers.

Ergas, Zaki, 1986, 'Reflections on Africa's Development', *Journal of Contemporary African Studies,* V, 1/2.

Gillies, David and Schmidt, [forthcoming] *The Challenge of Democratic Development: An Exploration,* Ottawa, The North-South Institute.

Gramsci, Antonio, 1971, *Prison Notebooks,* New York, International Publishers.

Greenberger, Robert, 1991, has warned in the *Wall Street Journal* (16 September 1991) there is just not enough money to pay off all the countries 'that now see the US as their model'.

Hutchful, Eboe, 1991a, 'Shades of Meaning: The Struggle to Define Democracy in Ghana', presented at the Annual Conference of the 'Canadian Association of African Studies', York University, Toronto, May.

Hutchful, Eboe, 1991b, 'A Perspective from Africa', *Reintegration of Eastern Europe and the Soviet Bloc: Implications for Developing Countries,* the North-South Institute, Ottawa, 25-26 September.

Hyden, Goran, Nzongola-Ntalaja, 1983, *No Shortcuts to Progress,* Los Angeles, University of California Press.

Laclau, Ernesto and Mouffe, Chantal, 1985, *Hegemony and Social Strategy,* London, Verso.

Landy, Joanne, 1991, 'Post-Communist Options: Can Western Progressives make a Difference?', *Peace and Democracy News,* New York, Vol. V, Summer.

Macpherson, C, B, 1973, Democratic Theories: Essays in Retrieval, Oxford, Oxford University Press.

Maynes, Charles, 1990, who describes the shift to democracy as 'another strategic gain for the United States', 'The New Decade', *Foreign Policy*, No. 80, p.4.

Price, Robert, 1984, 'Neo-Colonialism and Ghana's Economic Decline: A Reassessment', *Canadian Journal of African Studies,* 18, 3.

Sandbrook, Richard, 1985, *The Politics of Africa's Economic Stagnation*, London, Cambridge University Press.

World Bank, 1989, *Sub-Saharan Africa: From Crisis to Sustainable Growth: A Long-term Perspective Study*, Washington, November.

8. Democratic Transition in Africa: The Challenge of a New Agenda — Concluding Remarks

Jibrin Ibrahim

Africa is at a critical phase in its economic and political life, poised between the possibilities of democratic transition and development or political decomposition and regression. The notion of democratic transition implies a passage from a non-democratic to a democratic situation. In its essence, it is a question that can only be posed in the long term because the establishment of a democratic system, however defined, would constitute a veritable transition only if it becomes a fairly permanent feature of political life.

The essential attributes of democratic transition would include formal aspects such as constitutional rule and the operation of a multi-party system but also a more profound socio-political transformation that allows freely elected rulers and the majority of the civil population to impose their supremacy over ruling oligarchies of the military, ethno-regional blocs and/or the *nomenclature*. The call for a long-term perspective in no way belittles the fact that democratic transition has become one of the major political questions in the contemporary world, and most especially in Africa.

The African political scene has been shattered over the past decade by agitations for democratic transition. The period coincides with that of the collapse of communist regimes and the demands for democratic transition in Eastern Europe and the Soviet Union, and there is a tendency to see a causal link between political events in the two regions. Yet an active political opposition has existed in Africa long before the events that led to the fall of the communist regimes, so it is difficult to sustain the argument of the demonstration effect. Nonetheless, the two regions have suffered from similar types of authoritarian rule, and in both situations authoritarianism has run out of steam and could no longer be sustained.

Democratisation is the path of reason, history, hope and renewal. However, the continent has been subjected to such terrible forces of repression, exclusion and the destruction of her human and natural resources that anarchy, ethnic cleansing, warlordism and the decomposition of political communities remains a possibility for many African countries. That is the path of despair and hopelessness that must be averted. The way forward is the struggle for renewal in which democracy is a critical instrument that could lead to the reconstruction of politics and the state, culture, economic organisation and production.

Democratisation and the Crisis of Politics in Africa

Democratisation is on the African agenda because it has been denied to the people in such a systematic manner and for such a long time. Human rights are so urgently needed because the African person has been stripped of all rights and dignity. While certain Western scholars are laying ownership claims to liberty, democracy and human rights (Huntington 1993:40, for example), it is too easy for Western scholars today to forget the other side of their history — of slavery, of the inquisition, of colonialism and of the invention of genocide. All human beings who are subjected to the arbitrary powers of others seek release and relief from such powers. They seek freedom, a need that arises out of the deprivation of liberty. As has been argued by Paterson (1994:3), the West had nothing to do with the invention of freedom: all that was necessary was slavery.

Slavery had to exist first before people could even conceive of the idea of freedom as value, that is to say, find it meaningful and useful, an ideal to be striven for ... This was so because where there was no slavery all that human beings desired was to belong, to be mutually embraced and protected by those individuals and groups they knew and cherished; in short, to be bonded.

There is hope for Africa because its people have been in bondage and in deprivation for a long time and they see from their experience that salvation is in freedom — the freedom from authoritarianism, exclusion and underdevelopment.

Maybe Rousseau (1966) knew what he was talking about when he said citizens do not like obeying human beings, they prefer obeying laws. In the history of the West, democracy and human rights were placed on the agenda when extreme repression and economic hardship caused by excessive exploitation by the nobility provoked a general systemic crisis and the recomposition of society. The French Revolution, for example, evokes strong parallels with the contemporary situation in Africa because its basic reality was that the irresponsibility of a ruling oligarchy had created a scarcity of bread and a multiplicity of laws in the context of a generalised economic crisis.

This situation could produce two different results: first was the tradition of 'liberty, equality and fraternity' so eloquently expressed in the Declaration of the Rights of People and the Citizen of 1789. It led to the abolition of privileges, the assertion of the legitimacy of representative institutions, the rule of law, etc. The second tradition that grew out of the French Revolution was that of systematic repression and state terrorism. The political structure and capacity of the pre-revolutionary *ancien régime* was too weak to allow it fully to utilise its despotic powers. The reign of terror instituted in 1792-93 led not only to the excessive centralisation of the state, and to the postponement of the agenda for democratic transition until after 1871, but also to the systematic terrorisation of the population and one of the first modern cases of genocide in the Vendee region. Having consumed the royalty, the revolution turned on the revolutionary leaders and then on the ordinary people. The October Revolution, it should be recalled, was not the first to consume its children.

Authoritarianism

One of the major principles of political science is that although force is a central element in political systems, it cannot on its own sustain a polity. We are reminded by Rousseau that even the strongest is never strong enough to remain the master unless he is capable of transforming force into law and obedience into duty (1966:44). To rephrase Ian Fleming's imagery, unlike Diamonds, tyranny and authoritarianism can never be forever. Lucian Pye (1990:5) borrows from Karl Polanyi's idea of a 'Great Transformation' to announce that humanity has arrived at the historical point in which authoritarianism meets its Waterloo:

> The stigma of failure marks every form of tyranny, whether of the one man or the one party variety. As a result, profound changes have occurred in once-static authoritarian regimes, from those of generals and old-fashioned autocrats to the most advanced of the Marxist-Leninist systems. Dictatorial rule has failed to deliver on its promises of purposeful efficiency in all regions of the world.

We are thus at a turning point in world history, characterised by a general systemic failure of authoritarianism. Most authoritarian regimes are typified by stagnation and social decay, dilapidated infrastructure, run-down housing, shortages of consumer goods, poor agricultural production and declining life expectancies. In Africa, brute force and violence organised by the state has characterised widespread authoritarian rule. The object, says Achille Mbembe (1991:3) is not only to impose order and docility on subjects but also to terrorise the population in order to extort it.

The incursion of the military into African political life has further worsened the problems generated by authoritarianism. The military have impacted on society its anti-social and anti-political values. They have permeated civil society with their values— both the formal military values of over-centralisation and resolution of conflicts through repression and the informal *lumpen* values associated with the 'barrack culture' and the brutality derived from the colonial army.[1] The military have been trained to believe that power could be wielded and conserved on the basis of the force that resides within the military institution itself, and even those elements that have had access to higher education have remained at the mental level of 'barrack boys'.

The African military have remained committed to the erosion of civil relations and the banalisation of the culture of violence out of corporate self-interest, or rather, greed. Ever since the military realised that access to positions of power is a direct route to enrichment through the private appropriation of public resources, they have turned banditry into the means of the conservation of power. Although they have always claimed that the purpose of *coup d'états* was the fight against corruption, almost every military regime has turned out to be more corrupt than the regime from which it took over power. They have become the major segment of the power elite in most African countries, occupying the summit of the most powerful organisations in the polity and economy. It is a power elite that has a cultural and material stake against democracy, and yet one that has also created widespread consciousness that Africa can only survive and develop if authoritarian and military culture and control are combated by civil society and democracy is placed on the agenda.

Exclusion

The object of authoritarianism has been to exclude the people from the government and resources it controls. Most ruling oligarchies in Africa represented only a tiny fragment of their societies and a large majority was excluded from participating in the political process. According to Nelson Kasfir (1976:227), de-participation is the most striking feature of African political change since independence. The political arena shrunk as African states actively promoted de-participation by 'strengthening the central administration' and assuring the 'desuetude of participatory structures'. At the political level, the development of authoritarianism was rooted in what Peter Anyang' (1988:72) has characterised as the disintegration of the national coalitions that brought African countries to independence. The incorporation of kith and kin into ruling oligarchies and the exclusion of other groups from enjoying the prerogatives of power generated problems of ethnicity, clanism, regionalism, religious bigotry, and so on. Elaborate programmes of successive political exclusion (Ibrahim 1993) were implemented, and the vast majority of Africans lost their individual and collective rights to full participation in the political, civil and economic lives of their countries.

African political systems became increasingly characterised by the narrowing of the social and ethnic base of the 'President's men' and an expansion of the groups and segments of society excluded from the political process or significantly marginalised. The most affected groups have been women, the youth, ethnic and religious minorities (which could include marginalised ethnic or religious numerical majorities), and lumpen elements, products of ever-deepening economic, social and ecological crisis.

In Niger, for example, an elaborate system of monopolisation of power by a small ethnically based oligarchy emerged even before independence, and all rival political parties and trade unions were eliminated while the elite of the Zarma ethnic group, which comprises less than 20 percent of the country's population, had constituted itself into the sole ruling group. Between 1956 and 1990, for example, the top two office-holders of the country and over 70 percent of succeeding ministers were invariably Zarma. It required massive demonstrations, a general strike and the organisation of a national conference to destabilise this ethno-regional hegemony (Ibrahim 1993). Similar patterns of exclusion were established in other African countries such as Sudan, Nigeria, Mauritania, Rwanda, Angola and Somalia.

The various forms of exclusion posed fundamental problems related to the denial of equity and social justice, problems that led to the decomposition or near-decomposition of the said states. The Somalian case is a good example because despite the linguistic, religious and cultural unity of the people, the politics of exclusion succeeded in creating destructive divisions. The former dictator, Siyad Barre, who had usurped all powers in the country, used exclusion to terrorise the population. The only option left was that of armed resistance, and both the dictator and the people decided to use their most basic division, the clan, for mobilisation.

The ultimate problem was that once certain clans started monopolising positions in the army, civil service and business, leaving the others as domestic *lumpen* elements, the struggle for equity and justice developed in a climate where the monopolists were unwilling to compromise (Adam 1992:14). Gradually, repression and resistance were converted to warlordism as state institutions broke down and the law of the jungle (or maybe that of the desert), took over. All clans have by now both perpetrated and suffered from mass murder, torture and deprivation. Terrible memories that link clan identities to collective suffering have been ingrained in popular consciousness, and it will take considerable confidence-building measures for the Somali community spirit to be rekindled. The stories in Equatorial Guinea, Mozambique, Liberia, etc. are similar.

All societies are plural because human organisation is based on the cognition of different levels of identity — family, clan, village, tribe, religion, language, region, nationality. Pluralism in itself, however, is not problematic except when certain groups perceive that they are being excluded from what they consider to be their rights, whether religious, administrative, economic or linguistic. The central problem posed by exclusion is that of domination (Ibrahim and Pereira 1993).

Development

In 1988, the Chinese Academy of Social Sciences started a research project on the development of 'neo-authoritarianism'. Its aim was to 'modernise' Chinese authoritarianism along the lines of Korea, Taiwan, Singapore and Hong Kong, the so-called success stories in the promotion of economic development through authoritarian practices. Their inspiration was the American scholar S. P. Huntington, leader of the Social Science Research Council Committee on Comparative Politics (Pye 1990:17). This was probably the high point in the modernisation school's long-standing approach of advocating institutionalisation and political order (which they use as euphemisms for authoritarianism), as preconditions for economic growth in post-colonial situations. This thesis has crumbled under the weight of empirical evidence as the end-result of over thirty years of authoritarian rule has been significant economic underdevelopment in most African countries. Even the Americans have stopped arguing and struggling for the sustenance of authoritarian rule. The evidence of history has been unequivocal: tyranny has produced economic regression.

In this regard, Claude Ake (1990:2-3) correctly notes that under authoritarian regimes, the human being, the instrument and object of development itself, has been excessively abused:

> Repression has led to an enormous waste of human resources, the very engine of development. At the level of the community, people have been subjected to such arbitrariness and harassment that even their traditional capacity to cope has been undermined, and for the most part, many of them are in different stages of confusion, withdrawal, despair or silent revolt. On the level of the élite, the use of arbitrary coercion has turned Africa into a continent of refugees.

Indeed, repression has been so dehumanising that it is necessary to make a humanistic case for democracy even if it had no positive effects on development. Peter Anyang' (1988:86) adds that apart from the humanist argument which justifies democracy as a good in itself, a more instrumental case could be made on its behalf as there is:

> A prima facie case in the context of Africa of the post-independence period, to argue that where their has been more respect for democratic practices (however minimal) higher rates of growth and more successful models of accumulation have been ensured.

He concludes that the general rule is that lower levels of political participation lead to more intense forms of economic backwardness. In his response to Anyang', Mkandawire (1988:82) cautions on too much reliance on the instrumental case for democracy:

> (Development) is too precarious a concept on which to hang democracy. The struggle for democracy must be for democracy on its own right. This is not to deny that democracy may have instrumental value in the developmental process. ... I would rather see these benefits of democracy as windfall gains, albeit extremely important ones, given the wretched material conditions of our people.

Authoritarianism, as it were, has lost its last arguments at the empirical, instrumental and political levels. The next stage is to puncture its support base among intellectuals who have supported it on ideological grounds.

Democratisation and Ideological Labels

The end of the Cold War poses for Africa a political and intellectual challenge which provides a critical historical conjuncture to conduct a more fruitful debate and advance the struggle for expanding democracy in the continent. It is now possible to agree on an agenda of the expansion of democratic space as an immediate political objective, and few intellectuals would dissociate themselves from that objective today (Beckman 1989). There is, however, strong resistance among many intellectuals to going beyond standard cold war camps and labels represented by the dichotomy of bourgeois/liberal versus popular/people's democracy. The two basic labels, 'liberalism' and 'Marxism' are often more descriptive of ideological positions than sociological reality.

Labelling is partly a scientific (taxonomic) act of valuation, judgement and definition of a certain reality, and partly an act of stereotyping and imposition of prejudices. A basic feature of the sociology of labels is that once a labels sticks, its defenders tend to resist change even when the reality it is supposed to reflect changes. As a student of labels argues:

> Labels reveal more about the process of authoritative designation, agenda setting, and so on than about the characteristics of the labelled. Indeed it is part of our argument that labels mis-represent or more deliberately falsify the situation and role of the labelled (Wood 1985:352).

We all need labels to separate taxonomically our conceptions or convictions of the 'correct line' from the 'wrong line', but we must use them dynamically and know their limits. The time has come to revise our labels for the simple reason that the distance between the labels and the reality they are supposed to reflect is too wide, and often, attachment to the rigid dichotomies that labels define leads to serious political errors.

The book by Issa Shivji (1989b) on human rights in Africa is a good example. It is the archetype of the type of analysis based on a rigid dichotomy that presupposes a mutually exclusive existence between the so-called limited type of political and civil rights obtainable in liberal democracies and the social and economic rights that could be provided by a national democratic revolution (1989b:70). Shivji proposes what he considers to be a new African perspective on the question of human and political rights, which must be:

> Thoroughly anti-imperialist, thoroughly democratic and unreservedly in the interest of the people [and it] must distance itself openly from the imperialist ideology of human rights at the international level and cultural-chauvinist/developmentalist ideology of the compradorial classes, at the national level.

A more thorough democratic system is indeed necessary, but it is empirically wrong and politically irresponsible to reduce human rights to an imperialist project and to attack the 'liberal perspective' for placing emphasis on the civil and political rights of the individual. Shivji (1989b:72) proposes an alternative agenda based on two central issues, the right to self-determination and the right to organise. It is indeed true that democracy and human rights are the fruits of struggle and organisation, yet Africans cannot reject human rights simply because imperialist countries claim that human rights are necessary for Africans. Africans need human rights because they have suffered from and been fighting against the denial of these rights. The views of imperialists are secondary in this regard.

Furthermore, collective social and economic rights are important, but they cannot be opposed to or taken as an alternative for civil and political rights of individuals. It seems to us that the right to organise has in practice often been understood as the right to place and maintain Marxist-Leninists in power. The problem with Shivji's one-sided support for the Algiers Declaration of the Rights of Peoples is the refusal to take the African citizen seriously. Africa is not only populated by 'peoples', it is also populated by the individuals neo-Marxists so often dismiss. The label 'people' cannot be taken as an alternative for the reality of the 'individual', just as drawing attention to the pitfalls of liberalism should not lead to a rejection of its advantages; throwing away the baby with the bathwater.

The same could be said of Samir Amin's (1990:6) paper which restates a dictum so characteristic of a section of the left:

> The capitalist mode of production does not of itself require democracy but rather its characteristic oppression is hidden in economists (sic) alienation affecting the entire society. By contrast, the socialist project of a classless society freed of economistic alienation implies a democratic structure.

Amin had the good sense to suggest that socialist democracy has only been an implied rather than a lived reality, but he all the same insists that socialists have no lessons to learn from the recent crisis that has afflicted the socialist world (*ibid.*:6). Following the logic of Amin's argument, although the left has no lessons to learn on the question of democracy, it has lessons to give: 'the principal task is that of democratic re-politicisation of the masses' (*ibid.*:18). He also draws attention to the necessity of a debate on the role of revolutionary intelligentsia as a social catalyst capable of drafting a concrete alternative plan and promoting the struggles for its implementation (*ibid.*:19). The assumptions that the left is the 'pedagogue' of democracy and the implied meaning that democracy means putting Marxist-Leninist intellectuals in power must be questioned if the construction of democracy is to be taken seriously. As Esteve Morera (1990:24) argued, the first step in building democracy is the breaking-down of the one-way pedagogical relationship between intellectuals and the masses.

Intellectuals have never taught people democracy; people have fought for democracy from the standpoint of their lived experiences. As Mahmood Mamdani (1990:359) put it: 'Without the experience of sickness, there can be no idea of health. And without the fact of oppression, there can be no practice of resistance and no notion of rights'.

What we have called the crisis of labels is in fact a crisis of politics. According to Wamba-dia-Wamba (1992:1): 'we are in the process of a dominant historical mode of politics which have organised political processes since the 19th century'. He adds that in many African countries, politics itself had been made impossible through the excesses of authoritarianism. It is indeed a crisis of politics, understood in its more noble sense described by Bernard Crick, as the: 'Activity through which contending interests are conciliated, differences are expressed and reconsidered, the collective welfare ensured and the survival of the whole community protected' (Pye 1990:15).

Rather than sticking to conventional ideological labels and positions, it is more useful to consider the real effects of systems on real people. In his reassessment of leftist attitudes to democracy, Shivji (1989b) put his finger on the crux of the problem when he argued that intellectuals have always defined democracy from their 'label' of the class character of the state and its so-called ruling class rather than from the point of view of the people. As he expressed it:

> The moderates have a lot of faith in imperialism and the radicals have a lot of faith in the African state. What is common to both groups — and to the erstwhile African politician, militant or otherwise — is, virtually, a total lack of faith in the masses of the African people? (*ibid.*:12)

But then having faith in the people means not imposing a worldview and a programme on them. It means playing the democratic game. Who are the democrats and who are the non-democrats?

It is not excessive to claim with Immanuel Wallerstein (1988) that the bourgeois, i.e., the capitalist, has a historic role to play in modern society. It is not the oft-debated role of developing/underdeveloping the productive forces. The historical role of the bourgeois is to become an aristocrat. His objective is to extract rent and he is forced to accept surplus value only when the avenues for extracting rent are closed. Talking about revolutionary France, Blanning (1987:17) argues that:

> Whatever one's theoretical point of departure, it is clear that far from fighting the nobles, the bourgeois sought to join them. It was easy to do so — provided the aspirant had enough money.

The bourgeois is not a natural democrat because he knows that democracy imposes serious constraints on the extraction of rent. Given the propensity of intellectuals to dichotomous labels, the left gave a good label — 'democrat' — to an undeserving actor, the bourgeoisie, by insisting on the label of 'bourgeois democracy' for liberal democracy. Marxist-Leninists are not democrats (in the last analysis) because their politics is oriented towards the construction of a select vanguard party that will capture and exercise state power and build socialism for the people. Once Marxist-Leninists have power, they turn into despots because in their politics the control of state power by the select vanguard is more important than the people. It is not surprising that they persisted in calling dictatorial regimes people's or popular democracies.

Be that as it may, another lesson of contemporary history is that Marxists played a major role in building democracy in capitalist countries although they failed to do the same in socialist countries. The various struggles for extending the vote to the poor (defined as poor men) and then to women, for trade union rights, for the registration of *all* organisations (the base of democratic pluralism), for civil rights and for human rights were all conducted on broad fronts and often led by Marxists. When in the 1930s, capitalists got into trouble, they decided that if they kill democracy they might save their profits. Marxists were at the forefront in trying to save 'bourgeois democracy' during the Spanish civil war, the fight against Italian fascism and German nazism, etc.

It is indeed ironic that Marxists have been so blind to their own history— they helped build broad based, pluralist democracies against the wishes of the bourgeoisie and dismissed their own achievement as 'bourgeois democracy'. It should be pointed out, however, it was not only Marxists that participated in the building of democracy. The petty-bourgeoisie has also played a very important role. Beckman's (1990) position paper on interest group resistance to structural adjustment is very interesting in this regard as it correctly focuses attention on the contribution of professional petty-bourgeois groups to the construction of democracy in contemporary Africa.

It is necessary to outgrow the simplistic dichotomy and 'war' between bourgeois/liberal and proletarian/popular democracy. Liberal democracy historically started and developed in capitalist market societies, but there is no reason to struggle against its extension:

> The fact that liberal values grew up in capitalist market societies is not in itself a reason why the central ethical principle of liberalism — the freedom of the individual to realise his or her human capacities — need always be confined to such societies (Macpherson 1972:2).

The liberal democratic model, with its basic constitutive elements of regular governmental and legislative elections with universal and equal franchise, multiple parties, civil liberties, formal equality before the law and some protection for minorities is a good point of departure for the expansion of democratic space.

Democratisation and the Challenge of Survival and Renewal in Africa

The question of establishing, broadening and maintaining democratic space has become a central issue on the African agenda. The majority of Africans have been reduced to outlaws in their own countries by their own governments. After suffering all sorts of atrocities for so long, the threshold of tolerance has been broken all over Africa, and people are seeking ways of exercising some freedom from daily oppression. The result is increased agitation and popular demonstrations, strikes, protests and the like, aimed at the transformation of existing political systems. The success of the efforts towards democratisation will depend on the capacity of the African people to cope with a number of crippling challenges — imperialist control, the destruction of community, the 'Kalashnikov' factor, excessive corruption and waste of resources, and of evolving democratic systems that actually benefit the people.

The Imperialist Challenge: For African Control of African Destiny

Since the beginning of the 1980s, most African countries have been undergoing severe crisis. Most macro-economic indicators have been pointing downwards. The continent is not only the least industrialised part of the world, but is also undergoing deindustrialisation (Mkandawire 1991:80). Africa currently has the highest level of debt as a proportion of gross domestic product and is the only region where food supply is declining. As Colin Leys (1994:34) says:

> In sub-Saharan Africa most people are facing a future in which not even bare survival is assured. ... Out of a total population of about five hundred million, nearly three hundred million are already living in absolute poverty.

African leaders have played a major role in precipitating the crisis, but it is too easy to place all the blame on the continent's leadership. Since the mid-nineteenth century, the West has been decisive in directing the evolution of African societies. In the present day, the Western world has used the present African crisis, which arose partly out of its own activities and policies, as an excuse to justify tighter imperialist control of the continent and to use the international financial institutions to actualise this control.

Western intellectuals are busy painting the picture of a bifurcated world inhabited on the one side by Fukuyama's civilised 'Last Man' who is healthy, well-fed and pampered by technology while on the other is Hobbes' primitive 'First Man' living a life that is 'poor, nasty, brutish and short' (Kaplan 1994:60). Both Kaplan (*ibid.*:46) and Huntington (1993:22) raise an alarm — that Hobbes 'First Man' is returning the world to the epoch of constant war and barbarism that preceded the 1648 Peace of Westphalia when the modern nation-state emerged in Europe. In the words of Kaplan (1994:48), we are witnessing:

> The withering away of central governments, the rise of tribal and regional domains, the unchecked spread of disease, and the growing pervasiveness of war. West Africa is reverting to the Africa of the Victorian atlas. It consists now of a series of coastal trading posts, such as Freetown and Conakry, and an interior that, owing to violence, volatility and disease, is again becoming as Graham Greene once observed, 'blank' and 'unexplored'.

This racist Armageddon image of Africa, similar to the images that were painted in the nineteenth century to justify colonisation, is again being used to justify the argument that Africans cannot govern themselves, so a 'revival of colonialism' is needed on 'practical and moral grounds' to sustain 'the most basic conditions for civilised life'.

American scholars like Huntington (1993:27) have argued that we live in an era of a clash of civilisations in which the fundamental question is not which side you are on but what you are — Western or non-Western. He announces the end of struggles between princes, nation-states and ideologies and an impending world war which will occur along the fault-lines between civilisations. A New Menace is being invented to replace the 'Red Peril', and the West has chosen Islam as the new 'force of darkness' while alarmist propaganda is being produced about a 'Green Peril' (Hader 1993).

Meanwhile, the West has succeeded in imposing firm imperial control over much of the Third World:

> Global political and security issues are effectively settled by a directorate of the United States, Britain and France, world economic issues by a directorate of the United States, Germany and Japan, all of which maintain extraordinarily close relations with each other to the exclusion of lesser and

largely non-Western countries. Decisions made at the UN Security Council or in the International Monetary Fund that reflect the interest of the West are presented to the world as reflecting the desires of 'the world community' (Ibrahim 1993:39).

The West, with 800 million people constituting 15 percent of the world's population, has imposed its control over 85 percent or 4.7 billion people (Mabbubani 1993:13). The neo-imperialist control over Africa is deeper and more direct than for the rest of the Third World. International financial institutions (IFIs), in particular the International Monetary Fund (IMF) and the World Bank, have imposed Structural Adjustment Policies (SAPs) on at least 39 African countries. Heteronomy — government by external agencies — is the now African reality, with economic, social and political policies being developed and imposed by these agencies. Virtually all assessments reveal that the performance records of SAPs are very poor, partly because the policies are poorly designed but also because there is no local input and the foreign experts involved have meagre understanding of African economies (Helleiner 1994:10). While hypocritically calling for a return to pluralism in Africa, the West insists on solely dictating policies for Africa.

The establishment of democratic processes and culture in Africa is being seriously hampered by imperialist dictation.[2] Real democratisation must involve the elaboration and enactment of policies by elected officials. Democracy becomes farcical when national parliaments and executives cannot make major decisions on their own. In addition, the austerity component of the SAP packages is poisoning the political atmosphere by provoking popular protest and even insurrection by trade unions, students, professionals and broad layers of urban society (Harsch 1993:15; Bangura and Beckman 1993:76-81). The IFIs are calling for good governance in Africa, that African governments should consciously manage their regime structures in such a way as to enhance the legitimacy of the public realm (Hyden and Bratton 1992:7).

The policies being imposed, however, are so anti-people that they are eroding the legitimacy of even the recently elected governments of countries such as Niger, Benin and Zambia. However, the anti-people nature of the conditionality of the SAPs imposed on most African countries by the IFIs and the repressive state policies they provoke do serve to create a common African basis for analysis and the elaboration of strategies for combating authoritarianism and the expansion of democracy. The African people must regain control over their destiny if they are to make progress in the democratisation of the continent.

The Kalashnikov Challenge: For the Reconstruction of Political Community

The second challenge is that of the reconstruction of the African state. Notably in Liberia, Somalia, Rwanda, Mozambique and Angola, warlords involved in factional struggles for power have taken their countries to the level of decomposition or near-decomposition of state systems. Massive destruction of lives and property has occurred. The capacity for agricultural and industrial production has been destroyed and significant proportions of the population inhabiting the states have been turned into internal and external refugees. Civil war has not only led to mass massacres but is producing a generation that knows not peace, education, family values and civility; a generation bred in violence and knowledgeable only about force, fear and hatred. That is the Kalashnikov challenge, or acquiring the capacity for self-destruction.

In the intertribal wars of pre-colonial Africa, a week of combat between two communities might produce only two or three casualties. The dane gun had a quasi-democratic character. In one out of four times that the trigger is pulled, the gun explodes and the shooter is the victim. The Kalashnikov has changed all that. A young man with a single rifle could wipe out a whole village and start hate memories the whole of previous history could never have imagined. The destruction of state and society has become too easy and too frequent. A new word is entering the vocabulary of many African languages; in Somalia, Samatar (1994:8) informs us that it is burbur, the complete pulverisation of society. He draws our attention to the fact that: 'Without a workable state and its concomitant system of spatial and bureaucratic structures, no modern society can exist, let alone move forward' (1994:97).

Samatar's assessment of the Somali crisis opens a window of hope. The level of catastrophe and of civil disembowelment is so total that the only option left open is the politics of renewal and reconstruction.

A significant instrument for political renewal developed by Africans has been the emergence of the institution of national conference, a new social contract for the reconstruction of state and society. It was the Republic of Benin that showed the light that others have been trying to follow. Throughout 1989, workers, students and other popular forces were protesting against the monopoly of the state by the PRPB (Popular Revolution Party of Benin) and the monopoly of the party by the Kérékou clan. The people wanted a national conference in which they could demonstrate that the country also belonged to them. When the government called the conference in February 1990, its aim was to 'open up' the state to a few more people, with the tabled agenda of creating a national consensus by the elaboration of a new charter. The first decision of the 500 delegates invited to the conference, however, was to declare its independence from the government project and proclaim the sovereign character of its decisions over the party-state. The stage was set for the decomposition of the regime.

Since then, the national conference has become a politically infectious event, especially in Francophone Africa, and there have been persistent demands for it in numerous countries, including Anglophone ones such as Nigeria and Ghana. The objective of the convocation of national conferences has been to work out modalities for broadening participation in public affairs to all components of the nation.

In Niger Republic, for example, the 'black Friday' massacre of students on 9 February 1990, when at least 13 students were killed in a desperate attempt by the state to silence demands for popular participation, led paradoxically to the heightening of demands for a democratisation of the society. Adji (1991:333) argues convincingly that the thirty-year 'political freeze' imposed on the country since the suppression of the SAWABA party in the late 1950s was smashed on 16 February 1990 when demonstrators took to the streets on the call that 'those who massacre our children cannot consider us to be citizens of the country'. Adji adds that from then on, civil society was born in Niger, especially with the launching of *Haske*, the first independent newspaper in the country in June 1990 and the five-day general strike in November 1990 in which over 100,000 people demonstrated and demanded a national conference and multipartyism. The state was forced to accept multipartyism and the convocation of a national conference which took place from July to October 1991.

The idea of national conferences reflects a deep desire to reverse the process of de-participation that has been dominant in Africa since the attainment of independence. It is not, however, a panacea for democracy, it can only be a stimulus. Since Benin, the national conference has led to the overthrow of dictatorial regimes only in Niger and the Congo. In Gabon, Zaire, Togo and Cote d'Ivoire, the ruling oligarchies have been able to manipulate the national conference or ignore its injunctions and maintain itself in power despite the installation of multipartyism. Even the more successful democratic transitions such as Congo and Niger are under severe stress.

Be that as it may, democratic progress has been considerable as the monolithic power structures around most African presidents have been broken up in a majority of countries and the political system significantly opened out. The ideological battle has been won. Today, no African country upholds the ideology of one-party rule and only two— Libya and Uganda, are still advocating no-party systems (Sithole 1994:3). Virtually all other regimes on the continent are either operating multi-party liberal democratic models or promising to do so.

Corruption and the Pangolin Challenge: For the Common Use of Public Resources

Authoritarianism developed in Africa partly as a ruling-class weapon to protect neck-deep corruption; the ideologies used to sustain it were nationalism and socialism. The Zimbabwean example is eloquent in this regard. From 1987, socialism was used as an ideology to transform Mugabe from an ordinary prime minister with limited powers into an executive president who personally appointed 30 of the 150 members of Parliament; a Parliament he arrogated to himself the right to dissolve anyway.

Not surprisingly, Mugabe's notions of socialism led him to demand that all Pangolins captured in the country should be reserved for him. The Pangolin is a delicious mammal exclusively reserved for the consumption of absolute monarch in pre-colonial Zimbabwe (Mhlala 1990:225). Anybody capturing a Pangolin is expected to take it to the Monarch, and now to President Monarch Mugabe.

The Pangolin challenge is not really about delicious 'bushmeat', but about turning the state into free-range game. The struggle for socialism and national unity has been a cover for escaping accountability, as Sachikonye (1989) shows in his analysis of the 'Willowgate' scandal over Toyota Cressida cars. The Zimbabwean people protested massively against the spate of corruption and forced the Government establish the Sandura Commission which investigated the allegations (Austin 1989). A significant aspect of the 'Willowgate' crisis was that it helped checkmate Mugabe's drive towards one-party rule and thus assisted in broadening democratic possibilities in the country.

The struggle for democracy and the fight against authoritarianism is intimately linked with the anti-corruption crusade. The bane of African capitalism has been the excessive and destructive drive towards primitive accumulation that is threatening to kill the goose that lays the golden eggs. This is a creature of many names and concepts — for Mobutu it is Article 21 of the Constitution; for Jean-François Medard it is neo-patrimonialism; for Northern Nigerian politician Sabo Bakinzuwo it is *babakere*, 'the monopoly of eating'; for Richard Joseph it is prebendalism; for William Graf it is rentier capitalism, while for Max Weber it is booty capitalism. Whatever it is called, its effect is the erosion of state legitimacy because those who direct the affairs of the state are seen as serving their personal interests, with public resources, rather than standing over and above the immediate interests of the ruling class which both Marx and Weber associated with the modern state.

Excessive corruption prevents the emergence of a modern administration that could serve the long-term interests of an emerging capitalism. The deadly struggle of access to state power that is leading to political instability and civil wars is motivated by the compelling reality that those in power monopolise public resources for their kith and kin. It is impossible for all clans, factions, tribes, regions and corporations to have access to and monopolise public resources, and attempts by all to have access to state power can only lead to the pulverisation of society. The path of renewal is to ensure that those who hold public office are obliged to use public resources to serve public interests. The fight against corruption is at the heart of the struggle for democratisation.

The Challenge of Social Democracy: For Including the People in the Democratic Agenda

The current renewed interest in democracy all over the world, we repeat, is not the result of a change of fashion. It is a historical stage in the development of the human agenda. After Southern Europe and Latin America, dictators in Eastern Europe, Asia and Africa are being forced out of office or obliged to put democracy on their national agendas. After decades of telling 'their people' that strong one-party regimes are necessary for the preservation of national unity and for the promotion of economic development, many African dictators—including Bongo, Mobutu, Boigny and Kérékou—were all 'converted' to the virtues of multi-party democracy.

Of course we do not take these politicians seriously. What we take seriously are the forces that have forced them to declare allegiance to a system they have opposed so vehemently for so long. CODESRIA has become a major African forum for debating the challenge of democratising the continent.[3] The vigorous and flourishing debate has many participants, including Anyang', Mkandawire, Shivji, Gutto, Amin, Mafeje, Mamdani and Ibrahim. Despite the differences in the authors' positions, all could no doubt subscribe to a significant conclusion that could be summarised thus:

> that Africans should push forward the frontiers of democracy not only for instrumental purposes of promoting development or allowing the left to operate and not because democracy is good-in-itself, but because there is a universal human commitment to the improvement of the quality of human life, and democracy is one of these qualities. And that democracy should be pluralist and liberal as opposed to one-party or authoritarian.

The struggle for equality and the improvement of the quality of human life is a continuous one. The significant regression in gender rights and racial equality (over abortion, affirmative action for minorities, etc.) in the US and local government democracy and trade union rights in Britain are significant reminders that all clocks can be turned back, even if they are called established liberal democracies and even if we agree that they are a lesser evil. In the British case, Oldfield (1990) draws attention to serious demands for the enactment of a bill of rights that could save some of the country's 'traditional' civil and political rights from erosion. For example, one of the major factors that led to the Conservative victory in the 1992 British general elections was the disenfranchisement of a large section of the poor and Labour supporters who had not paid their poll tax.

Democracy should be considered to be a space that can be reduced at any time, and it requires consistent struggle to maintain and expand it.

Democratic transition has not been easy and cannot be easy. There is too much at stake. For the president's men, there is the loss of power, privilege and the wealth that has been and is being accumulated from the state. For all those excluded from power, there is the promise of a better tomorrow. For both sides, the stake is worthy of a major battle. In many African countries, the democratic movement is strong enough to impose its agenda of democratic transition in spite of strong ruling-class opposition. The national conference is a good example of the people's capacity to establish a forum for organising resistance against corruption and authoritarianism, against the wishes of those in power (Diop and Diouf 1991:8). Since the Benin National Conference, which took the regime by surprise, many of the other leaders —Boigny, Mobutu Sese Seko, Bongo, Paul Biya—have built up more guile in thwarting the objectives of or preventing the convening of other conferences. Their determination to remain in power cannot be unconnected to the will to preserve their vast personal fortunes.

An important issue on which the debate about democracy in Africa should focus is citizenship, irrespective of how old-fashioned and how 'liberal' the concept seems. The birth of the citizen is the first step in the construction of democracy. There cannot be democracy without democrats, and the historical democratic actor is the citizen. Citizens are not born out of declarations or constitutions; they emerge when simple individuals are empowered to exercise civil, legal, political, economic and religious rights. The era of great theoretical battles between advocates of individual rights and advocates of collective rights is over. Citizens need collective rights to adequate health facilities, education and a living wage. They also need the freedom of speech, assembly and association as well as the right to vote and be voted for, freedom from arbitrary arrest, the right to fair trial and the right to worship as they deem fit.

The citizen as an effective actor can only exist if civil society exists. Civil society is a part of society that has a life of its own, which is distinct from the state and fairly autonomous from it. According to Shils (1991:4), the idea of civil society has three main components:

- The first is a part of society comprising a complex of autonomous institutions — economic, religious, intellectual and political — distinguishable from the family, the clan, the locality and the State.
- The second is a part of society possessing a particular complex of relationships between itself and the State and a distinctive set of institutions which safeguard the separation of State and civil society and maintain effective ties between them.
- The third is a widespread pattern of refined civil manners. The third aspect has not been much emphasised in the current literature on civil society. For civil society to exist, the conduct of members of society towards each other must be characterised by civility. Polished and refined manners are expressions of respect for other members of society. It is a precondition for democratic practice as citizenship cannot be effective if the rights and the dignity of the person are not respected (Ardigo 1985:49).

Part of the African tragedy is that refined and civil manners which are essential elements of socialisation in most traditional societies have been eroded by state terrorism, war, hunger and parochial politics of authoritarian leaders, and people are losing respect for their neighbours. Citizenship, it should be recalled, cannot be exercised in situations of war and terrorism (Leca 1986:175).

Another important attribute of civil society is that it is necessarily pluralist. On the one hand, there are the partially autonomous spheres of economy, religion, culture, intellectual and political activity which operate in their domains. On the other, within each sphere, there is a multiplicity of partially autonomous corporations and institutions that operate independently (Shils 1991:9). This plurality is a major factor in the maintenance of the relative autonomy of civil society from the state. It also helps in providing favourable conditions for democratic practice.

The central political problem has been how to spread freedom (meaning empower the people) in a socio-economic context in which the dominant economic class composed of a tiny minority controls most of society's resources. Morera (1990:33) presents the problem succinctly:

> The greatest problem for a theory of democracy is that the split between the dominant class interested in preserving the status quo, and the progressive coalition, bent on changing it, presents a limit to consensus. It is not to be expected that those with power will relinquish it voluntarily, and hence methods other than consensual ones, what Gramsci refers to as force, may become necessary at some point.

This is the theoretical basis that justifies revolutionary politics, as the dominant class will not willingly give up power. The sociological problem posed is that revolutionary politics has not led to a democratisation of social and political life in socialist countries, contrary to the expectations of the revolutionaries and their fellow travellers.

The problem is usually referred to as that of 'real existing socialism'. Since the democratic credentials of existing socialist societies were so weak, the left has usually spoken of democracy from the standpoint of what the theoretical situation ought to be rather than the sociological reality in countries that legitimated their regimes with the ideology of Marxist socialism. Those that knew 'real socialist' societies to be 'fake socialists' insisted they could not be integrated into 'real Marxist' analysis precisely because they were fake. And those who knew 'real socialist' societies to be 'genuine socialists' even if they had some shortcomings refused to address themselves to their democratic records and took the simpler route of writing eulogies about their achievements in industry, health, education, and so on — eulogies that have been revised today.

The left had no real debate on democracy. A long time ago, before Lenin invented democratic centralism as the correct organisational form for all revolutionaries and banned factions, tendencies, minorities (Mensheviks) and of course other parties, there used to be a debate about social democracy. The idea was simple, to extend the frontiers of both socialism and democracy. If we are to take Etienne Balibar (1974:71) seriously, Marxist mistaken articles of faith could be rectified. His argument is beyond reproach. In their preface to the 1882 Russian edition of the *Communist Manifesto*, Marx and Engels argued that so much political and economic transformations had occurred over the twenty-five years since they wrote the manifesto that if they were to rewrite it, there would be multiple revisions. They decided not to revise so as to leave the historical document intact. Today, more than a century later, it seems that in Marxist theory and action fidelity to historical documents has remained more important than responding to historical realities of our time.

Having said that, the reality is confused by the fact that social democracy, in its various historical forms, is just another label. It refers to a wide range of systems from the revolutionary agenda of Marx and Engels to the Scandinavian (and in fact European) form of negotiated mediation between the logic of capital and that of redistributory justice. As Beckman (1990) points out, contemporary Western social democracy has developed in a context of corporatism, a system that weakens pluralist democracy on the one hand and incorporates interest groups and trade unions into the logic of capital on the other.

Nonetheless, the rapidly growing debate on corporatism and the attempt to define civil society has focused attention on a significant issue. In general, pluralism and autonomy of interest groups promotes the growth of democracy. In Western Europe democracy is advanced when the social democratic consensus is broken and interest groups are able to regain some autonomy vis-à-vis the logic of capital. Gramsci was the first to discover this phenomenon when, following the Turin strikes of 1919, he realised that trade unions were simply incorporating workers into the logic of capital. That was why he called for the development of autonomous factory councils.

French national statistics published in March 1990 revealed that while workers were able to significantly improve their relative strength and increase their real incomes under the conservative decade 1970-80, their relative strength and real incomes declined considerably under Mitterand's socialism between 1980-90. To put it differently, Lenin's workers got into trouble the moment they had to give up their own interests to serve the socialist state.

On the Expansion of African Democratic Space

In the 1950s and 1960s, in most African countries, democracy was sacrificed on the altar of national unity and/or socialism before it was really tried. It is therefore wrong to assume that it failed, rather it was never given a chance (Sithole 1994). After three decades of the negation of democracy, the current African conjuncture is characterised by increased popular struggles for the expansion of democracy and the consequent crumbling of authoritarian ideologies and practices.

Some issues have been more or less resolved: authoritarianism has failed in its promise to build the African nation-state and develop the economy; the military has failed in its promise of imposing order and fighting corruption; the concentration of power in one party or one absolute president has failed to produce hegemony. The African people have shown that they are for plural democracy. At the same time, we are witnessing the elaboration of new structures and processes of the neo-colonial control of the African people and their resources under the Structural Adjustment Programmes imposed by the IMF and World Bank in collaboration with African governments which, despite protestations to the contrary, are reinvigorating the ideology of repression.

This paradoxical situation sets a new research agenda of the development of new approaches, concepts and methods in the struggle for democracy based on consultation with popular forces and interest groups. The objective is the broadening of popular participation in responsible and responsive government in an environment in which citizens enjoy broad civil, political, social and economic rights. The development of citizenship rights should be at the centre of the democratisation process, a sort of return to primary sources in the debate.

Construction of Citizenship and Overcoming its Weaknesses

Citizenship is an important notion because it defines the constitutive elements of the democratic state and elaborates the relationship between state power and individuals. According to Malcolm Waters (1989:160), it spells out procedures and sets of practices defining the relationship between the nation-state and its individual members. Citizenship implies not only the erosion of the arbitrary use (misuse) of state power but also the movement away from what has been called 'pro-forma democracy', in which 'formal citizens' are directed by so-called mass parties, national single parties, national liberation movements, etc. to act in particular ways defined and imposed by autocratic leaders. It seems to us that democracy should be about the rights of citizens to live their own aspirations and programmes.

The problem of citizenship is that although it sets out the conditions of formal equality, it also structures and institutionalises socially reproduced inequalities. Waters (1989:174) argues, for example, that in capitalist societies:

> Citizenship atomises society into multiple sovereign individuals and reintegrates them into a nation. Unequal class or status relations are denied and a structure and ideology of common objectives are superimposed.

The state, however, intervenes to regulate the atomised individuals into labour markets that serve the interest of capital. In the Soviet Union and Eastern Europe, the existence of privileged individuals in the nomenclature and ruling party meant that:

> Dominating political interest groups are in principle able to dictate differential relationships between the state and individual members of civil society which constitutes virtual unequal citizenship. The substance of a 'partocratic' hierarchy of this sort is not merely political prestige, or power, it is material. The three main political strata have differential access to the material resources of the state (Waters 1989:169).

The development of feminist discourse and struggle has also drawn attention to the ways in which human and civic rights are not gender-neutral. Civic equality, for instance, often translates as discrimination against women who have less time and resources to participate owing to additional domestic burdens that tie them down and the non-remuneration of much of the work they do (Phillips 1991:44). It means that women do not enjoy the same real rights, privileges, autonomy and power even when they have formal equality (Sow 1994:7).

The construction of citizenship therefore implies the continuous struggle against the privileges which certain classes and groups enjoy because of their control of resources and/or power.

In Africa, people have suffered the indignities of being forced to address themselves as citizens (in Zaire, for example) or comrades (as in the Congo) in situations in which they enjoyed no citizenship rights and were being treated as subjects and in very uncomradely terms. The essence of the democratic movement is that people are struggling to give real content to some of these labels.

One major problem in promoting citizenship rights in contemporary Africa is that a significantly high percentage of Africans are migrants and are thus not citizens of their countries of residence. The case for migrant workers has been eloquently put by Mamdani in this volume:

> The outcome of migrant labour is a radical rupture between the land of one's birth and the site of one's labour; and as a result, between the country of one's citizenship and that of one's residence. Since 'human rights' in liberal theory flow from membership of a political community (citizenship) and not of a labouring community (residence), this single fact has been sufficient to strip millions of migrant labourers of their human rights.

In this case, therefore, citizenship serves to disenfranchise large groups of people. In addition to the case of migrant workers, the numerous civil wars in different parts of the continent are producing increasingly larger numbers of political refugees who do not enjoy citizenship rights. Ecological crisis and famine are other factors that elongate the list. Africa is being transformed into a continent of refugees and orphans. Mamdani's solution to this problem is to struggle for residency rights rather than citizenship rights for migrants. We would prefer the extension of citizenship rights to all residents who accept them, so the human person rather than the nationality of the person becomes the major factor.

In all possible instances, the frontiers of democracy should be broadened. The sense in which we use the notion of the expansion of democratic space is tied at one level to the reduction of the nuisance produced by those who control state power and economic power. At another level, it involves the struggle for concrete power gains by democratic actors. We are advocating that the individual and collective rights of citizens are taken seriously.

Taking People's Rights Seriously

The expansion of democratic space develops on the basis of the empowerment of citizens as well as groups in society, be they ethnic, religious, regional, clan, etc. To put it differently, it means inverting the trend of the criss-crossing network of:

1. Oppression — the monopoly and misuse of power by a minority. We have to develop strategies that will enable citizens to monitor and push back the frontiers of authoritarianism.

2. Exploitation — unequal exchange in relations of production and in the market and monopoly of resources — the struggle for a more equitable distribution of socially created wealth.
3. Discrimination — unequal rights and treatment on the basis of an incident of birth such as gender, religion, caste, language or ethnic group.

In so doing, we need to develop:

Civil Rights

The liberty of the person, freedom of speech, thought, movement, assembly, association and faith, i.e., the maintenance of human rights and the rule of law, and the empowerment of women, youth, peasants, ethnic and religious minorities and other surbordinate groups.

Political Rights

The right to participate in political activity, voting and competition for political office. These rights are enhanced by the pluralism of political organisations, political parties, mass media, trades unions and professional organisations.

Social and Economic Rights

The right to economic welfare and security (health, education, living wage, etc.). This must include the prevention of the monopoly of public resources by a minority of central planners or 'free marketers'.

Notes

1. In most African countries, the term 'barrack person' suggests someone who is crass, uncouth, uncultured, rough and violent. The military institution has entered the African psyche as a socially and culturally destructive element.
2. At the Nairobi Reflections on Development workshop in September 1994, Thandika Mkandawire, executive secretary of CODESRIA, called the World Bank and the IMF the last Stalinist institutions of the twentieth century. He reports, for example, that in Benin, Mali and Senegal the world bodies insisted that their negotiations with the governments were secret and details should not be released to national Parliaments.
3. CODESRIA has held two major conferences on the issue, and there are research networks on social movements and democratic struggles and on democratic transition. In addition, the organisation's periodicals, *CODESRIA Bulletin* and *Africa Development*, have published a number of thought-provoking articles and polemical comments on the issue.

References

Adam, H, M, 1992,'Somalia: Militarism, Warlordism or Democracy', *Review of African Political Economy*, 54.

Adji, Souley, 1991, *Logiques socio-communautaires et loyautés politiques au Niger*, thèse, université de Bordeaux II.

Ake, Claude, 1990, 'The Case for Democracy', African Governance in the 1990s, The Carter Centre, Emory University.

Amin, Samir, 1988,'Political Instability and the Prospects for Democracy in Africa', *Africa Development*, 13.1, 13.3.

------------, 1990, 'The Issue of Democracy in the Contemporary Third World', paper for CODESRIA Symposium on Academic Freedom, Research and the Social Responsibility of the Intellectual in Africa, Kampala.

------------, 1993, 'Reply to Jibrin Ibrahim', *CODESRIA Bulletin* 2.

Anyang' Nyong'o, P, 1987, (ed.), 'Popular Struggles for Democracy in Africa', Zed Books, London.

------------, 1988, 'Political Instability and the Prospects for Democracy in Africa', in *Africa Development*, XII, 1:71-86 and XII, 3:83-87.

Ardigo, Á, 1985, «Sociabilité et démocratie», in J, Leca and R, Papini (eds.), *Les Democraties: Sont-elles Gouvernables?*, Paris, Economica.

Austin, R, 1989, «Néo-colonialisme et corruption: le scandale 'cressida' au Zimbabwe», *Politique africaine*, 36:118-124.

Balibar, E, 1974, «La rectification du manifeste communiste», in *Cinq études du matérialisme historique*, Maspero, Paris.

Bangura, Y, 1986, 'Structural Adjustment and the Political Question', *Review of African Political Economy*, 37.

------------, 1989, 'Authoritarian Rule and Democracy in Africa: A Theoretical Discourse', UNRISD, Discussion Paper, 18.

Bangura, Y, and Beckman, B, 1993, 'African Workers and Structural Adjustment: A Nigerian Case Study', in A, Olukoshi (ed.), *The Politics of Structural Adjustment in Nigeria*, James Currey, London.

Beckman, Bjorn, 1989, 'Whose Democracy: Bourgeois Vs Popular Democracy' *Review of African Political Economy*, 45/46:84-97.

------------, 1990, 'Structural Adjustment and Democracy: Interest Groups Resistance to Structural Adjustment', SAREC.

------------, 1993, 'The Liberation of Civil Society: Neo-liberal Ideology and Political Theory', *Review of African Political Economy*, 58:20-33.

Blanning, T, 1987, *The French Revolution: Aristocrats Vs Bourgeois*, Macmillan, Houndmill.

Dahl, Robert, 1994, 'A Democratic Dilemma: System Effectiveness Vs Citizen Participation', *Political Science Quarterly*, 109, 1.

Diop, M, C, and Diouf, M, 1991, 'Statutory Political Successions: An Afterword', *CODESRIA Bulletin*, 3: 8-9.

Garrett, M, 1970, *The French Colonial Question: 1789-1791*, Negro University Press (Reprint), New York.

Gutto, Shadrack, 1988, 'Social Revolutions — The Preconditions for Sustainable Development and People's Democracies in Africa',*Africa Development*, XIII, 4:89-103.

Hader, Leon, T, 1993, 'What Green Peril?', *Foreign Affairs*, 4.

Harsh, E, 1993, 'Structural Adjustment and Africa's Democracy Movements' *Africa Today*, XV, 4.

Helleiner, G, K, 1994, 'From Adjustment to Development in Sub-Saharan Africa', Mimeo, Toronto.

Huntington, S, P, 1993, 'The Clash of Civilisations',*Foreign Affairs*, 3.

Hydem, G, and Bratton, M, 1992, *Governance and Politics in Africa*, Lynne Rienner Publishers, Boulder.

Ibrahim, Jibrin, 1986, 'The Political Debate and the Struggle for Democracy in Nigeria', *Review of African Political Economy*, 37.

------------, 1990, 'Succession Politique et crispation sociale au Nigéria: 1987-1988', *Année africaine*, CEAN, CREPAO, Pédone, Bordeaux.

------------, 1992, 'From Political Exclusion to Popular Participation: Democratic Transition in Niger Republic', in B, Caron, A, Gboyega and E, Osaghae (eds.), *Democratic Transition in Africa*, CREDU, Ibadan,.

------------, 1993, 'History as Iconoclast: Left Stardom and The Debate on Democracy', *CODESRIA Bulletin*, 1, pp.22-23 and 'History as Iconoclast: A Rejoinder', 2, 17-18.

------------, 1993, 'Transition to Civil Rule: Sapping Democracy', in A, O, Olukoshi (ed.), *The Politics of Structural Adjustment,* in Nigeria, James Currey, London.

Ibrahim, J, and Pereira, C, 1993, 'On Dividing and Uniting: Ethnicity, Racism and Nationalism in Africa', paper for International Development Information Network, CLACSO, Buenos Aires.

Imam, A, 1985, 'Ideological Manipulation, Political Repression and African Women', AAWORD occasional paper series 2.

Kaplan, Robert, 1994, 'The Coming Anarchy', *Atlantic Monthly*, February.

Kasfir, N., 1976, *The Shrinking Political Arena*, University of California Press, Berkeley.

Leca, Jean, 1986, «Individualisme et Citoyenneté», in P, Birnbaum and J, Leica (eds.), *Sur L'individualisme*, Presses de la Fondation Nationale des Sciences Politiques, Paris.

Leys, Colin, 1994, 'Confronting the African Tragedy',*New Left Review*, 204.

Mabbubani, K, 1993, 'The Dangers of Decadence: What the Rest Can Teach the West', *Foreign Affairs*, VXXII, 4.

Macpherson, C, B, 1972, *The Life and Times of Liberal Democracy*, Oxford University Press, Oxford.

Mafeje, A, 1993, 'On Icons and African Perspectives on Democracy: A Commentary on Jibrin Ibrahim's Views', *CODESRIA Bulletin*, 2:19-21.

Mamdani, Mahmood, 1990, 'The Social Basis of Constitutionalism in Africa' *Journal of Modern African Studies*, XXVIII (3):359-374.

Mbembe, Achille, 1991, "Désordres, résitances et productivités", *Politique africaine*, XXXXII, 42.

Mhlaba, Luke, 1990, «Le retour du Pangolin: les réformes politiques au Zimbabwe», *Année africaine*, CEAN, CREPAO, Pédone, Bordeaux, 1990.

Mkandawire, T, 1988, 'Comments on Democracy and Political Instability', *Africa Development*, Vol. XIII:5-31.

------------, 1991, 'Crisis and Adjustment in Sub-Saharan Africa', in D, Ghai (ed.), *The IMF and the South*, London, Zed Books.

Moreira, E, 1990, 'Gramsci and Democracy', in *Canadian Journal of Political Science*, XXIII, 1.

National Consultative Forum on National Conference, 1990, *Agenda for Democracy*, Lagos.

Nyang'oro J, E, 1994, 'Reform Politics and the Democratisation Policies in Africa', *African Studies Review*, XXXVII, 1.

Oldfield, Adrain, 1990, 'Citizenship: An Unnatural Practice', *The Political Quarterly*, VXI, 2.

Ossebi, Henri, 1992, «Production démocratique et transition post totalitaire au Congo», paper for CODESRIA General Assembly Conference on Democratisation Processes in Africa, Dakar.

Paterson, Orlando, 1994, 'Freedom, Slavery and the Modern Construction of Rights', lead paper for conference on Democracy: Popular Precedents, Practice, Culture, Johannesburg: University of the Witwatersrand, July.

Phillips, Anna, 1991, *Engendering Democracy*, Polity Press, Cambridge.

Pye, Lucian, 1990, 'Political Science and the Crisis of Authoritarianism', *American Political Science Review*, VXXXIV, 1.

Rousseau, J, J, 1966, *Du contrat social*, Flammarion, Paris.

Sachikonye, L, 1989, 'The Debate about Democracy in Contemporary Zimbabwe' *Review of African Political Economy*, No.45/46.

Samatar, A, I, (ed.), 1994, *The Somalia Challenge: From Catastrophe to Renewal*, Lynne Rienner, Boulder.

Sandbrook, R, 1988, 'Liberal Democracy in Africa: A Socialist-Revisionist Perspective', *Canadian Journal of African Studies*, XXII, 2.

Shils, Edward, 1991, 'The Virtue of Civil Society' *Government and Opposition*, XXVI, 1.

Shivji, Issa, 1989a, 'The Pitfalls of the Debate on Democracy' *CODESRIA Bulletin,* 13, IV.

------------, 1989b, *The Concept of Human Rights in Africa,* London, CODESRIA, Dakar.

Sithole, M, 1994, 'The Democratisation Process in Africa: Is the Second Wind of Change Any Different From the First', paper for CODESRIA/Rockefeller Reflections Workshop, Nairobi, September.

Sow, Fatou, 1994, 'The Role of Gender Analysis in the Future of Social Sciences in Africa'. *CODESRIA Bulletin,* 2.

The IMF and the South, London: Zed.

Wallerstein, I, 1988, 'The Bourgeoisie as Concept and Reality',*New Left Review,* 167.

Wamba-dia-Wamba, E, 1992, 'Africa in Search of a New Historical Mode of Politics', paper for CODESRIA General Assembly Conference on Democratisation Processes in Africa, Dakar.

Waters, Malcolm, 1989, 'Citizenship and the Constitution of Structural Social Inequality', *International Journal of Comparative Sociology,* XXX, 3-4.

Wood, G, 1985, 'The Politics of Development Policy Labelling', *Development and Change,* XVI.

Achevé d'imprimer
sur les presses de l'Imprimerie Saint-Paul, Dakar
Juin 1995